RELENTLESS

Chronicles of Faith, Love and Service

RALPH & DONNA HOLLAND

RELENTLESS

Chronicles of Faith, Love and Service
*First Edition - **Ralph & Donna Holland**, 2021. 250p. - 6x9*

ISBN 97987566695946

1. Christian Life. I. Title
CDD 248.5

Address:
P O Box 270996
Flower Mound TX 75027-0996
drrholland@gmail.com
imndonna@gmail.com

Interior Design and Cover:
Richy Mugni
losmugni@gmail.com

Printed in USA

TABLE OF CONTENTS

CREDITS

Paul said to Timothy, "I thank Christ Jesus our Lord, who has given me strength to do his work. He considered me trustworthy and appointed me to serve him," (1 Timothy 1:12)

We relate and identify with what Paul said, without pretending to have reached his level of apostleship, but with gratitude to the Lord for having called us to serve Him – especially and particularly as missionaries to the nations.

In appreciation . . .

- To our parents who never opposed our pursuit of the calling upon our lives.

- To the mentors in each phase of our lives.

- To our sons and daughters-in-law, and our grandchildren that have been supportive and encouraging along the way.

- To our late daughter for so willingly adapting to so many living situations . . . and enjoying the journey with us.

- To our colleagues that God has used to enrich our lives and given us the opportunity to walk with in so many different cultures.

- To our followers who have insisted that we write these chronicles.

- To all of you who have honored us by reading through these pages and thus walking with us through many unforgettable experiences.

- To **Omar and Cristina Herrera**, colleagues in the ministry, who along with their team, have helped us compile these chronicles. With understanding and skill, they have helped us tell our story, not just so that the readers can be inspired, but also challenged. The motivation is to glorify the Lord through this book full of faith, love and service.

We are *grateful* . . .

PROLOGUE

Many times, when we have shared some of the hundreds of experiences in our ministry life, we have been told, "You should write a book." The truth is that we have been very reluctant to do so, simply because we have never wanted to give the impression that our lives have been anything special or better than that of so many others and their service to the Lord. We can do nothing without Christ and His direction in our lives. The only thing that has mattered to us is to accept and do the Will of God unconditionally in every step and decision. To that purpose we have dedicated and spent our lives.

We resisted the idea of a biography or history of our lives. However, when it was suggested that we write our story as "Chronicles," it seemed like a good option and a viable way for us to share our steps, processes, occurrences, experiences, and the life-lessons that we have lived and learned along the way in our service to the Lord.

Paul said, "Don't you realize that in a race everyone runs, but only one person gets the prize? So run to win! All athletes are disciplined in their training. They do it to win a prize that will fade away, but we do it for an eternal prize. So I run with purpose in every step. I am not just shadowboxing." I Corinthians 9:24-26 (NLT)

With this paradigm and conviction, we have lived and served. Everyone has their unique purpose, their calling and talent, with which they live and for which they will be accountable to the Lord one day with the hope of hearing the Lord say, "Well done, good and faithful servant." With that in mind, we share another counsel from Paul, "Hold firmly to the word of life; then, on the day of Christ's return, I will be proud that I did not run the race in vain and that my work was not useless. But I will rejoice even if I lose my life, pouring it out like a liquid offering to God,] just like your faithful service is an offering to God. And I want all of you to share that joy. Yes, you should rejoice, and I will share your joy. Philippians 2:16-18 (NLT)

Our hope is that every believer would desire this same counsel from Paul. It is a joy to serve the Lord! For that reason, and with that motivation, if we can share something that would encourage and motivate others to serve the Lord in a Relentless manner, it will be worth it to have shared our life-lessons and what we have learned in the process. Why? Because everything that you will read in these pages represents a life poured out in living sacrifice. (Romans 12:1)

Many times, we have been asked how one can know the will of God for their life. With confidence, in that we have lived it, we can share with you from Proverbs 3:5-6 (NLT): "Trust in the Lord with all your heart; do not depend on our own understanding. Seek his will in all you do, and he will show you which path to take."

We thank God that, more than 53 years ago, He joined us in marriage with the same desire and determination to do His perfect will. We pray that these stories which we share here in the form of chronicles will be a blessing in your life. How sad it would be to get to the point of death and realize that one has never lived. For that reason, we continue forward, **Relentless**, as some have described us.

Ralph & Donna Holland

INTRODUCTION

Someone said, "it's not just about living, but about giving purpose to your life." It is easy to think and say what you want to do, but the challenge is to do it. In all matters of life, one encounters this reality. Many live, but not all do so according to what God determined for them. When we have the privilege of encountering certain people who live and who also know the purpose for their life, the result can be none other than admiration and inspiration.

The story of Ralph and Donna Holland is much broader than what has been written in these pages. Their lives consist of hundreds of personal, family, and ministerial experiences, many of which are related throughout these inspiring chronicles lived by them in different countries, circumstances, and times. It will be noticeable that there are no elitist stories here, nor anything like "everything has been perfect for us." On the contrary, everyone will quickly discover that they have been invited to read parts of their life as a whole. They do not avoid sharing the efforts -- and the achievements. The laughter -- and the tears. The mistakes -- and the successes. Health, illness, and death. Courage, determination, and obedience, despite everything, will inspire you as you read through this work.

You have in your hands a dramatic and exciting telling of unconditional obedience to God and His calling. Even in times of great need, they continued to serve God with passion, faithful to their calling. This is a telling of their years of tireless service, of love for God and the mission that was born in their hearts from a very young age.

You are welcome to join them on their journey. You will go with them on their adventures in missions in the Caribbean, the Americas and beyond, to Asia and Africa, and passing through Europe. Always obedient, always happy, always Relentless, and ready for a new adventure of faith, love and service to the Lord.

Then you will not become spiritually dull and indifferent. Instead, you will follow the example of those who are going to inherit God's promises because of their faith and endurance.
Hebrews 6:12 – (NLT)

"Jesus, Use Me, Lord please don't refuse me . . . "

Jesus, use me,
Lord, please don't refuse me.
Surely there is a work that I can do.
Even though it's humble,
Help my will to crumble.
Though the cost be great,
I'll work for you.
Dear Lord,
I'll be a witness if you will help my weakness.
I know that I'm not worthy, Lord of thee.
By eyes of faith, I see you
Upon the cross of Calvary.
Dear Lord, let me your servant be.
And, if it be thy will Lord to go across the seas
Lord, help me to be willing to say "yes."
Jesus, use me, please, Lord, don't refuse me.

As sung by Ralph and Donna. Engaged and married. With piano, accordion, guitar, clarinet, or saxophone. The same song, same commitment, same call, same determination.

"No one has the right to hear the Gospel twice until everyone has heard it once."
Oswald J. Smith

PART 1

CHILDHOOD

DONNA

SEPTEMBER 1949

I am very proud to tell everyone that I am from the state of Oregon, in the northwest of the United States. Its beauty is indescribable. Its mountains, lakes, coasts, and rivers make it unique. But, although I'm from there, I wasn't born there. Oregon is the land where my parents were born. After World War II, my dad decided to prepare to serve the Lord in ministry. He made the decision to study at a Bible college in Tupelo, Mississippi.

When he graduated, he was immediately appointed as part of the staff for the same Bible college. At noon on September 21, 1949, I was born. The unique detail is that it was his first day as the Dean Registrar, and he had to register all the students. But, in the midst of that process, I came to interrupt his life. I was born on his first day as dean. Early in my life, he served as Dean Registrar of a Bible college in Tupelo, Mississippi, and then later as President of another Bible college in Portland, Oregon. His last day as President of that Bible college turned out to be the eve of my wedding.

So, from the day I was born to the day before my wedding, my dad was involved in Bible college work. As you will read, these extremely formative years of my life were greatly impacted by the opportunity to know so many people.

Being a "campus brat," I had the privilege of making new acquaintances each year as students gathered on campus, visiting ministries came by, and so many awesome mentors influenced my life.

My parents named me Donna which in its Latin form means "Doña," that is, "the owner and administrator of the house." It is rather unique that I have lived up to the significance of that name through responsibilities that I have assumed using my administrative skills.

Many have identified my gift as a teacher, and I do not doubt it. When I share the Word of God, I feel that it is where my ministry flourishes most. From the time I was born until the day before I got married, I lived in an atmosphere of "learning" which was a privileged preparation for the gifts the Lord has given me.

An interesting detail is that, while living in Portland, I met Ralph, my husband, when he came to Oregon to study. He was from the south of the United States. In fact, he lived remarkably close all his life to the area where I was born. So, I understand a little bit of the southern culture of the United States, although I identify more with the northwest.

As for my father, besides the fact I was born on his first day as dean of the Bible college, at the time, he was also starting a new church, preaching open air on a rural farm property. So, I arrived just in time to also interrupt that endeavor which he continued to pastor for a few years before returning us to Oregon.

FAMILY LIFE

Without a doubt, the origin of my family and the environment in which I was raised had a lot to do with the direction of my life. My dad and mom were very disciplined and hardworking people. With them there was no room for laziness; they demanded a disciplined life, not only in terms of home life, but in all of the disciplines of life. When I entered school, the discipline was rigorous. As a child, there were times when I would wake up in the morning and not feel particularly well, so I would tell my parents, "I feel a little sick." Then they would say, "Go to school and upon arrival, if you still don't feel well, we'll pick you up." Only on a few occasions did they actually have to pick me up. However, as hard as it sounds, I learned this lesson: Most of the time, if you put forth an effort, you can make it!

Relentless, the title of this book, describes that early training by my parents. Because of a consistent work ethic in our home, being tired was not an excuse to slack off of our work. Today, I do not resent the insistence on "plowing through" despite being tired. It was this training that has, without a doubt, been a vital part in shaping my character into who I am today.

As a young girl, I started looking for a summer job. I wanted to have my own money to buy my clothes since we did not have a lot of financial resources. Although our needs were always met, I wanted to work. In Oregon, there are farms, especially strawberry farms in the area where I lived. And although I lived in the big city of Portland, it was common that at the end of school young people would go to those farms to work and earn extra money during the two or three weeks of harvest. Later in the harvest season, the currant berries also ripened, and that was another good opportunity for me to earn a little extra.

I remember my dad warning me, "If you start, you'll have to work until you finish the harvest." I assured him that I would. However, on the second or third day, I was so sore from bending over to pick berries that I wanted to quit the job. Early each morning, my parents would knock on my bedroom door, "Donna, get up!" When I would respond with "my back hurts!" their answer was non-negotiable: "Donna, you started, so you must finish." That was the discipline that was ingrained in me.

A school project marked a significant moment in my development. When I was in fourth grade of elementary school, one of my teachers asked my father to become more involved in the process of my education, considering that the degree my dad earned in college had to do with child development. The teacher claimed that I was not doing everything I could, and that I could achieve much more.

Given that encouragement by my teacher, my dad took the time to sit down with me to prepare a report. We had to choose a state to write about, so I chose my birth-state of Mississippi. I had to research encyclopedias; I had to search and find very specific details. He worked alongside of me, teaching me how to prepare a good report. From then on, until I graduated from high school, I was the top student in my classes, and graduated as valedictorian of my high school class. Yes, it all started that night when my dad took that time to sit down with me and teach me how to prepare that report with excellence. That shaped my life. From then on, I didn't just want to get an "A," I wanted the best "A" in the class, the best grade! If not, I felt like I had failed. While I possibly became an extremist in this area, I think my desire for excellence helped shape many areas of my life bringing great fulfillment – and made me Relentless.

Although my parents were demanding and expected us to reach as far as we could, they were also very affectionate. They did not lack in affirmation or recognition of my achievements. For example, if I came from school with a report card with several "A's" and maybe a "B," my dad would say, "Why a "B""? But then he would laugh and congratulate me on the good grades. The truth is, Dad had his way of always pushing a little for greater results, but at the same time he always affirmed and celebrated what we achieved in life.

It was my dad's custom each night to come to mine and my brother's rooms (I only have one sibling), and before I could fall asleep, he had to tuck me in, arranging the blanket as only he could do. A little kiss on the forehead and I was fast off to sleep. This is a very special childhood memory.

My mom was also affectionate, but in perhaps a shyer way. She was a very humble woman and an excellent homemaker. Yes, the love in our home was warm and embracing. Even in my mother's shyness and limitations, her support for my father's call was special. Not only in the ministerial tasks, but also in everything that had to do with our lives. Without question, the rather extreme work ethic and disciplined culture in our home had a lasting impact in my upbringing, development, and my training.

LITTLE IS MUCH

I cannot say we lived in poverty because we always had what we needed. But there was no extra money for non-essentials. My dad, being part of a Bible college, and dedicating his life to ministry during my childhood, did not have a big salary. In fact, most of my life, we lived on the campuses of the colleges where he served, both in Mississippi and Oregon.

At one point, he and my grandfather were finally able to build us a house. I was about thirteen years old. The college, at times, experienced a shortage of funds. My Dad would defer his income to help the college through difficult times. Often, he would only receive around $50 for fuel expense since our housing and food were provided on campus.

During those lean times financial times, I remember, really without resentment, that I only had one dress to wear every time I went to church. For school, I needed to have three changes of clothes! Thank God, a friend of mine, who was one size larger than I was, began to pass her clothes on down to me. Also, my step-grandmother, who worked cleaning houses for wealthy people, often was given clothes from their children as giveaways. Of course, she passed those on to me! The truth is that I was rarely able to wear a new piece of clothing actually chosen and purchased by me in a store. At the start of each school year, I was allowed to buy two new dresses and one pair of shoes that had to last me all year. Other than that selection by me, I always settled for what was given to me. I think it taught me my first lessons on how to live a life totally given to God and what it is like to live with little. And that is precisely what we had to do in the beginning of our work as missionaries: live with little.

When I look back at my childhood, I have no complaints; I have no regrets. I realize that my experiences were particularly important in my training. Some of my dad's colleagues criticized him for not having a home of his own and for not having another job with which he could provide much more for his family. I do remember him working for the postal service during the Christmas holidays so that they could give us gifts. I also went along with him and my brother in a little newspaper distribution business. My mother worked in a hospital for several years to contribute what she could to the family budget. I believe that the faith and dedication that they lived was much more important than any material blessing that they could have given us.

However, the college, where my father served, one day considered everything that had not been paid to him, and it was then they gave him a large sum of money. With that, he bought a piece of land. And there, with my grandfather, they built our first house. They took 18 months to build that home from the foundation to the roof. The only part of that construction that they did not personally do was to install the furnace system; and they didn't do that because the installation came with the cost of the furnace. No way would they pay to have something done that they could do themselves. I have not forgotten everything I learned from construction, as I often worked alongside them. Indisputably, all these experiences made a wonderful contribution to my life, and from all of them I have been able to draw experience and understanding.

FAITH IN THE HOME

A very interesting fact, and part of my legacy in missions, is that my paternal grandparents were missionaries in Alaska before my dad was born. Between 1918 and 1920, my grandparents and their first two daughters went to Alaska to serve as missionaries, which was not yet part of the United States. It was a new frontier to conquer with the gospel and there they went. A few years later, in 1923, my dad was born. My parents were married in 1943, and one year later, the U.S. Army drafted my father as a soldier. These were times when there was no choice; so, towards the end of World War II, he was sent to Burma and India as part of a battalion that was to keep the peace in that region after the war. He was the chaplain's assistant, which gave him many opportunities to visit small churches and thus move among believers in Burma and India.

One night in India, Dad was on a mountainside begging the Lord to call him to missions. The Lord said to him, "You will not live as a missionary in another country, but you will train and be very involved in sending others as missionaries." And in fact, that is what he did! The Bible college where my dad served was renowned for training and sending more missionaries than any other. He, of course, taught the "Missions" class.

When he resigned from the Bible college staff, he went to the headquarters of his denomination to work in the Department of Foreign Missions after serving for a time as a Regional Director. So, for a time, my parents lived in Ecuador as a supervisor of missionaries, and then back to the USA as Secretary of Foreign Missions for his denomination. These two life-callings on my father represent two fundamental areas in my formation:

1. The Bible college. It was there that the passion as a "teacher" of the Word became a part of me.

2. His ministry as an administrator in missions. They tell me that I excel in the gift of administration, which came from his influence.

On the other hand, my mom was a noticeably quiet woman with a stutter when using certain words. Her mother died when she was five years old, so she lived with a single dad until she was nine years old. At that time, her father married again, and by the age of sixteen, she chose to go live with my dad's sisters. They were some of her best friends. The closeness of the two families gave opportunity for my parents to know each other better which led to their marriage.

It is worth saying that the state of Oregon is known for having very disciplined and industrious people. My grandparents were no exception as they were business owners and industrious people. These are people who did not miss any opportunity to work. They lived a work ethic... that work ethic was planted in me and has made me Relentless.

The decisions my parents made to serve the Lord full-time, even with few resources, had its rewards. God rewarded them for those sacrifices they made, and they ended life very comfortably, having more than enough. Their lifestyle was never luxurious, but they lived well. Their houses and cars were very tasteful, and being frugal, they were able to leave an inheritance for my brother and me. But more than just material things, it was all a sign of God's faithfulness. When one learns to put the most important things first and still go through some moments of scarcity for God's sake, He does not fail. We not only observed the faithfulness of God in their life, but have learned that for ourselves as well. That is why, when Ralph and I entered missions, those seeds were already sown in my heart. Our sacrifices and God's faithfulness were already part of my understanding and my surrender to God.

During my adolescence and youth, I had the opportunity to meet many people. In that we lived and worked on the Bible college campus, it gave me many opportunities to travel, and to meet and welcome visitors to our home. I remember many times I had to vacate my room because we were visited by a missionary, a pastor, or an evangelist. I was happy and honored to get to provide my room for them to stay with us.

Because of so much entertaining of guests, I learned from my mom how to cook and participate in other homemaking activities at a young age. My mom was a seamstress, and she made my clothes as well as hers. When I was eight years old, I wanted to learn to sew, but my mom said, "Better not, you're going to run your finger under the needle and you're going to hurt yourself." But my father had another view of the matter, so he said, "It doesn't matter, if she gets hurt, she will heal." So, I learned to sew and for my eighth-grade graduation I wore the dress I had made myself! It was made from a very complicated pattern and design; I still remember it, and I'm still proud of it!! When I wanted to learn how to iron, the same thing was repeated. My mom would say, "She's going to burn herself," and my dad would say, "If that happens, it will heal."

By my twelfth birthday, when my mom came home from work, I had the table and food ready for dinner, that many times included guests. I remember well our apple tree and a particular season when all the apples ripened at the same time. The question I asked myself was "What are we going to do with so many apples?" I couldn't think of anything better than making pies. I made thirteen apple pies in one day and put them in the freezer to eat during the winter! All this was part of my training in diligence, work, and the discipline that I carry today in my life.

Among so many people who visited our home, there were

always many missionaries whom I admired. I listened to their testimonies and their reports. I remember one day when I was looking out the kitchen window at the garden while washing dishes, and I felt a powerful call to missions that I could not resist. During those days, we had a missionary lady from Liberia, West Africa in our home. I was standing at the window and trying to figure out how to convince my parents to allow me to go back with her to Africa. I wanted to go to the mission field, now!

The only "condition" I put on the Lord was that He work out "what to do with the snakes" in that I was terrified of them. I am still terrified of them! Later, the Lord, with His good sense of humor, first called us to Puerto Rico, the Dominican Republic, Haiti and the Caribbean Islands where there are no snakes! Why? Because years earlier, they brought in a little animal called a mongoose that can even whip a cobra; that's why there are still no snakes on those islands. Yes, I believe God heard my only condition!

In my adolescence, I was always very devoted to the Lord. From the age of thirteen my decision was to serve Him in missions or wherever He sent me. In different time periods, my dad was pastor of three different churches and president of the Bible college, so I was always involved and challenged in the service of God. I remember that in one church, we were a very small group of only three young people in the group, but the three of us were very devoted to God. That was special in an environment that didn't lend itself to spiritual commitment.

Most think of the United States as a Christian country, where all children go to Sunday school and are raised in church. But the part of the country where I was raised was the most secular, the least Christian state in the union at that time. As a result of this mentality, I learned to share my testimony in the secular school environment where I attended and trained myself to stand firm in my beliefs in front of the students and teachers, many of whom were atheists. How they made fun of me! The whole class knew I was a Christian! But I stood steadfast in my faith. I also know that this was part of my training for missions.

TEEN-AGE YEARS

I have observed that children who are raised in pastors' homes and in the church from birth often have not had a radical transformation in their lives when they receive the Lord. This is perhaps a result of seeing and doing the same thing every week: church, worship, sermons, and Christian programs. From doing so much of the same, some may end up getting so used to it that the possibility of a real and transforming encounter with the Lord Jesus Christ seems unlikely.

But my testimony does not conform with that line of thought. When I was six years old, I was in one activity of the many that took place in the church summer camp in Bend, Oregon that was different. Why? Because I found myself responding to the Lord's call on my life. I walked to the altar with conviction and ready to make a decision. That night, in that simple place and in one more service, there was a big difference. That evening, I received the baptism of the Holy Spirit. What an experience! A wonderful transformation of my life! I remember when I got up from the altar, I felt like I was walking on air, that all the colors looked brighter than ever. Everything had changed! Not that at that age I was a great sinner, but I knew that I had just been born again in a tender, exciting, dramatic, experience. The next day, I was baptized in water in the Deschutes River. Since that time, I have lived the life of salvation and faith, without any doubt in my mind and my heart, because of the wonderful transformation that took place in me on that occasion. It was not difficult for me to live in a secular culture. I was in an environment of schools that made fun of and mocked Christianity, but that made me stand firmer in the faith and learn to defend what I believed more fervently.

Yes, I lived a very healthy adolescence and youth, very devoted to the Lord. From a young age, I served in the church in any area I could. Serving in the Kingdom of God was my passion and my decision. I participated in everything. I went to many youth camps, and the truth is that I was always one of the most devoted among the girls. I loved prayer, seeking God in those powerful moments, and I don't regret that. I realize that I put down strong and deep roots from my youth. I played the clarinet in the church orchestra. If there were new people at the altar, I was always ready to pray with them. I started teaching Sunday school when I was fifteen years old. We didn't hesitate to go evangelize door to door, although sometimes I went with a lot of fear. Sometimes I would knock on the door and pray that no one would answer, because I didn't want to talk to strangers. But I knew that was part of the church's evangelism program and I felt a commitment to participate. Yes, this too was forming my character and unconditional service to the Lord.

RALPH

THE SUMMER OF '47

The summers are hot in Tennessee in the month of July. Another year of the same experiences, the same tasks, the same routines of country life. But although everything seemed the same, it wasn't. On this day, in a humble two room wooden house, in the outskirts of a small town of 200 inhabitants, a place called Enville, I was born. I was the second child. My brother was 14 months older than me. I surprised my mom by coming a little earlier (almost a month) than she anticipated. My dad was away at work in the neighboring state. Life was slow paced, simple, and quiet in a community with no doctor, no clinic. So, my grandmother played the role of a mid-wife to help usher me into the world. Just a few short minutes after my birth, she wrapped me in some blankets and took me to her house about a quarter of a mile up the road. She and my grandfather had a grocery store in their living room. And of course, there was a scale to weigh the meat and the produce they sold. So, she placed me on the produce scale so she could record my birth weight which the house-call doctor, who arrived three days later, would enter in the record for my birth certificate.

My ancestry is mostly British, some Irish and a little Swiss-German. My mother named me Ralph simply because she liked that name even though there was no record of anyone in my ancestry that bore that name. I like to think that it was by divine guidance that she gave me that name. It had to do with my purpose in life. I always dreamed of being a medical doctor and, although I never attained that dream, I feel that I have been a doctor for the soul for thousands of people. When you combine my first name with my second name, you come up with Ralph Leon, a combination that was only used when my mother was scolding me for my mischief. I like the Biblical connotations of my two names: Ralph is Raph in the Hebrew meaning the God who heals; Leon is the word for "Lion." Jesus in me is the Lion of the tribe of Judah. So, the Jesus in me is the healer of souls.

Indeed, I was born in a rural community. I grew up around animals, farming, hunting, fishing, and typical country-life customs. There were both benefits and limitations living in the rural south. Our house was small. Mom cooked on a wood-burning stove that served the dual purpose of cooking and heating the house. We had no indoor plumbing, so water was drawn from a well. And down a path away from the house was our "outhouse." Now those of you from the tech generation that don't have a clue, ask your grandparents what that is. We kept a Sears and Roebuck catalogue in the outhouse also. Your grandparents can fill you in on that "detail" also.

It is very typical for one to either have pleasant memories of your childhood, the customs, the lessons learned or to loathe with resentment having been brought up in difficult circumstances. I choose the former. Great memories. Great experiences. Work ethic. Gratitude and respect. That upbringing played a very important role in the shaping of my character and preparation for my purpose in ministry. I learned to be grateful for little. For "little is much" when God is in it.

LIFE WITH LITTLE

By most standards, my parents were poor. But their work ethic was consistent; hard work was engaged in enthusiastically every day. Love, creativity and need made things work. My mom had a degree in education. But her teaching assignment was a one-room school that housed first through eighth grade all in that one room. And she taught them all. My mom traveled by horseback to the school to teach her lessons. I am inspired as I think of the sacrifice that she and my dad made to provide for our family. Lives were impacted by their sacrifice. At least my life was impacted.

Living in rural settings, we did the tasks that were necessary. I chopped wood for kindling for cooking, drew water from the well, picked cotton, even tried my hand at plowing, and helped on the farm as needed. Yes, I am a hillbilly.

My father operated heavy equipment to dredge riverbeds. He also went to school at night to become a "part-time" mechanic. If that was not enough, he worked the late shift at a diner in a truck-stop as a "short-order cook." Finally, he landed his dream job when he became a Highway Patrolman. During his career, he was elected County Sheriff for a term and later returned to the State Patrol where he retired.

Living next door to my grandparents, I had the opportunity to go fishing with them on many occasions. As I mentioned earlier, my grandparents had converted their living room to a grocery store. In addition to the store, my grandfather built a mobile grocery store on his truck and would drive throughout the community selling anything from cheese to chickens, live ones at that, from his "peddling" truck. It was fun to run the route on the peddling truck with my grandfather.

Wow, do I have some memories!! One childhood memory was when my father bought two goats, which he would harness to a little wagon. My brother and I would then walk along the highway with the goats and wagon collecting discarded coke bottles that had been thrown in the ditch along the way. Then we would cash them in at the grocery store for about 2 cents per bottle. Plastic bottles and aluminum cans for soft drinks had not been invented at that time. (I must be old).

My childhood was lived in an environment of love, respect, work ethic and family unity. I became who I am and will never forget that I grew up with great blessing. The blessing of family.

FAITH AND FAMILY

Faith in God was priority in our home. Even though my father was raised in a Christian home atmosphere, he was not a born-again believer until later in his adult life. As a matter of fact, Donna and I were married and serving on the mission field in the Caribbean when the news came of the glorious conversion that my father had experienced. His words to me on the phone were, "Ralph, you've got a new Dad." And indeed, the scripture bore true, "...in Christ you become a new creation, old things pass away, all things are made new." My father was a great Dad and never opposed our active church life and would even attend services frequently. He would tell my mom to be sure and pay the tithe on his paycheck each month. When one invests in the Kingdom and raises his children in the Christian faith, sooner or later, conviction will draw that person to make a personal decision for Jesus Christ. That was the case of my father.

Admittedly, our church denomination was a traditional group that was considered strict and somewhat legalistic in some of their beliefs. Of course, some of us really needed rigid guidelines. My mom was the spiritual anchor in our home. Her life was marked and directed by prayer. Her relationship with God was so pure and perceptive that she didn't have to catch us kids in our mischief. She perceived by the Spirit when we were doing something wrong or just plain mischief.

In that my dad had eight brothers, I have a lot of cousins. One of the memories of my youth, which I will never forget, was our quartet. Two of my cousins, and my brother and I, formed a singing group. Not only did we sing, but we played musical instruments. So, we would sing a verse and play a verse of the songs in our repertoire. In my humble opinion, our instrumental abilities were way beyond our singing abilities. Cousin Monette played the piano (keyboards didn't exist) and was very accomplished. Her brother, Larry, played the trombone. My brother, Stanley, played trumpet and I played the clarinet. What awesome memories! We traveled around the area singing and playing in many special church activities sponsored by different churches.

Those were wonderful days! Unique memories of my youth.

I left the life of sin at the age of 8. I received Jesus as my Savior in the Sunday school class. I realized the need for water baptism and the infilling of the Holy Spirit. Soon after, I was baptized in a lake near our city.

One of the highlights of my youth was our summer camp. Youth from all over the state would gather at our campground for a week of spiritual saturation with hundreds of young people. These were powerful experiences, true revivals of the soul where renewed commitment to the Lord took us to a deeper place in Him. I always played my clarinet in the orchestra for the services. Thankfully, for that talent, I received a partial tuition scholarship to the University of Tennessee.

So numerous were the experiences lived in my youth which without a doubt helped shape my character and guided me toward my purpose.

My brother, who is 14 months my senior, was 6 feet, 7 inches tall. I was one of the shortest students in my classes all through high school. I actually grew two inches after I started college. My height made me self-conscious. I tried to overcome that complex of being, as my brother called me, "Shorty," inserting folded cardboard in my shoes in hopes that I would appear taller. I stretched, jumped, hung from things and prayed in an effort to be taller. But soon I would learn, it's not about how tall or short you are, but rather how big you allow God to be in your life and live out your purpose.

GOD GOES TO THE MOVIES

When I was about 14 years old, I wanted to hang out with my school friends. Every Friday night they would all go see a movie at the local cinema. They invited me. Going to the movies was an activity that was forbidden by our church at that time. This particular time, I really wanted to go. So, the challenge was to devise a plan to meet them at the movies without my parents knowing. We came up with the clever idea that I would tell my mother that my friend, Harold, was having a birthday party at his house. And then from there, Harold's father would take us to the theater. Sounded like a plan. So, I proceeded to tell my mom that I was invited to Harold's birthday party. My mom said we would need to take a birthday gift to the party. But since it was not really his birthday, I told my mom that we didn't need to buy a gift because he didn't want gifts at his party. Tell me what 14-year-old kid is going to say, "No gifts at my party!" That was the first hiccup in my story.

Nonetheless, Friday arrived, and mom took me to Harold's house. It was raining. I mean really raining. So much so that mom questioned if the party would still happen. I assured her that the party was on! We arrived at Harold's house. All the lights in the front of the house were off. Of course, no one else had arrived at this non-party. I continued with my lie and said, "Everyone is in the back of the house, I'll knock, and they will let me in." I got out of the car and dashed through the rain to the house. I waved my mom on. She cunningly went to the end of the street and turned around to pass by the house again. I had entered the house; Harold said that his dad was ready to take us to the movies, so we had to run to his car. I insisted on using the bathroom to give time for my mom to pass by the house and return home. We jumped in Harold's dad's car. He let me ride in the front seat. I noticed headlights coming up behind us. and I was sure it was my mom, so I needed to duck. Of course, Harold and his dad would not understand why I needed to duck. I began to examine the add-on air conditioner that had been installed under the dash (AC in a car was uncommon at that time). The car passed. All was clear. Off to the movies.

When Harold and I arrived at the movies, several of our friends had already saved our seats. The lights were still on in the theater. We were all excited that our deceptive plan had worked, and now I was in the forbidden place for my first movie. As I sat there, I began to feel ill because of lying to my mom. I told my friends that I needed to use the bathroom before the movie began. I was delayed in the bathroom for a long time, so Harold came to see about me. I told him I was sick. And I really was. I was not physically sick, but my emotions were a wreck due to the lies I had told. I told him I was leaving. I ran to the corner drugstore (that was called an Rx back then) to borrow their phone and call my mom to pick me up. Still raining. Clothes were soaked.

I called my mom, and soon she was there to pick me up. She asked how I had gotten to the pharmacy and why there, why didn't I wait at Harold's house. Still not ready to confess, I told her that Harold's dad had taken everyone there to be picked up by their parents and that the party was cancelled. I went silent. Mom glanced at me with loving eyes and said, "Ralph, you lied to me, didn't you?" But the issue didn't end there. She added something that still resonates in my ears to this day: "Ralph, when I returned home, I got on my knees and was praying until you called." Overwhelmed by what I had just heard, I broke down, confessed, repented, apologized, and thanked my mom for praying. Then mom added, "Yes, I knew that the Lord was going to talk to you and that you would repent, so I wasn't surprised by your call."

What an experience! It was not about the religious prohibition of going to the movies; it was about the deceptive lies and the work of the Holy Spirit in my life. Beware of thinking that you can deceive Mom and the Holy Spirit!

A DREAM AND AN AIRPLANE

I was a dreamer. I always dreamed of a life beyond the limitations of my environment to something greater. Living in the country as a child did not give much hope of a world beyond the rural farmlands. That did not stop me from dreaming. One day, as a barefoot boy running and playing in the field with my friends and my brother, we heard the unusual noise of an engine that only occurred maybe once a month. An airplane. Vintage. Maybe a DC-3 or similar. You could hear it for miles away given the absence of noise in the calm countryside. We shouted, "Here comes a plane! Here comes a plane!" Even the adults would leave their humble houses to witness a glimpse of the sophisticated life beyond the country. As others watched in awe, I dared to declare, "Someday, I'm going to fly in one of those planes." Those around scoffed and laughed reminding me that I was just a boy from the hills of Tennessee. My dream was alive. That day came. Up, up, and away. For the last 15 years I have logged flying an average of around 150,000 airmiles annually to 103 nations of the world. You would think by now I should own stock in the airline.

Dream big. God is faithful. He keeps His promises and fulfills the desire of our hearts as we obey, worship, honor and follow Him, even on an airplane.

RELENTLESS

COLLEGE MAJOR – MAJOR CHANGE

On Sunday morning, just two weeks prior to my start at the University where I would begin my studies to become a doctor, I was enjoying another one of our blessed church services in my home church. As our Pastor finished his message, he was prompted by the Holy Spirit to invite those who desired to gather around the altar and pray together.

As I knelt on one of the altar benches, God and I began to converse. It was a profound moment in His presence. A moment that turned into almost an hour. I was lost in His presence so much so that I was oblivious to who remained around the altar. By this time most of the attendees that Sunday had left the auditorium, but not my dear mother and some close family friends. And of course, my Pastor was close by. God was speaking. I was resisting. But God always wins. I surrendered, lifted my hands toward the heavens and at the top of my voice, screamed, "Yes Lord! Yes, Lord!" My Pastor came close, kneeling beside me and with an assured voice said to me, "Ralph, God has called you to dedicate your life to ministry." There was no doubt. Because I was already registered to attend the University of Tennessee for a year, I followed through with that and then transferred to Bible college in Portland, Oregon.

PART 2

COURTSHIP

A PHONE CALL

Every story is unique, much more so if it is a love story. Every detail, every circumstance is loaded with feelings, memories, emotions, and life decisions. It was no exception in Ralph and Donna's romance story. Ralph was very social, naturally friendly and enjoyed the company of others. It was when he entered Bible college in Portland, Oregon, that he met Donna. He had attended the University of Tennessee for a year, then decided to transition to Bible college in Portland. It is important to remember that Ralph is a southerner. Being from the state of Tennessee, his southern accent was very heavy, which is why many times the people of the northwest had a hard time understanding him.

Donna is two years younger than Ralph. During the summer prior to her senior year of high school, she worked as a secretary in the office for her father, the president of the Bible college. Even though she was just sixteen years old, she was very mature and responsible. Having grown up on the Bible school campus gave her an understanding that was advantageous for her assignment. Among her duties was the review of the new student applications and to register them for the upcoming school year. Ralph decided to enroll as a new student at the Bible college. However, he had not yet submitted his application for the fall semester, even though that was his plan.

During those years, young men were eligible to be drafted into the army. Certain exemptions were given to those who were university and seminary students. A friend of Ralph's family was part of the board that recruited soldiers for the U.S. Army. That board member let Ralph's father know that he was on the list to be drafted. This was during the time of the Vietnam war. Immediately. Ralph called the Bible college, and it was Donna who answered the phone. To qualify for exemption to the draft, he had to submit a letter of acceptance from the Bible college where he would be attending.

When the phone rang, she was away from her desk, and had to run down the hall to the office to answer. On the line, she heard the voice of a young man from the state of Tennessee, with a heavy, typical Southern accent, so much so that Donna had a hard time understanding him.
As she noted the details of their phone conversation, she was sure that he had said his name was "Ronald Holland." Ralph began to explain his dilemma, "Look, I have my documents ready to send to you to be registered and approved. If I don't submit a letter of acceptance to the draft board before their Monday night meeting, they're going to draft me into the army." In those days, there was no email nor cell phone service. No, none of that. There was only the postal service. However, they had a special system of immediate delivery. So, at the request of the unknown applicant, Donna responded by saying that she was going to do her best; although, truth be told, she was a little upset by the fact that the young man had not submitted his application on time.

So, Miss Donna Judd prepared the necessary letter. Donna's father signed the letter and off it went "special delivery," arriving just in time for the Monday evening meeting. But the story doesn't end there. The director of the board that selected the future soldiers, noticed that there was an error in the name; the letter read Ronald Holland instead of Ralph Holland. "Ralph, I guess they are referring to you," the director said, "but I must have another letter that corrects the mistake and thus exempts you from being drafted into military service."

This is how, by phone, Ralph and Donna met for the first time. Ralph again phoned the school office to requested a new letter with his name corrected. Donna was not impressed by this young man from Tennessee. She did not understand his accent and even when he told her his name, she was still sure that he had originally said "Ronald." But he defended himself by saying, "How am I going to tell you that my name is Ronald when by such a mistake I could go to the Vietnam War?" Finally, the exemption from the army came and Ralph was able to enter the Bible college in September 1966.

The arrival of that new student was very special. That day, Donna was there, curious and attentive, to see "that guy from Tennessee with such a heavy accent," Ralph came in, she saw him and said to herself, "Humm, he looks better than I imagined," although he didn't capture her attention. She was not overly impressed. She had imagined that he would be a humble country boy, ugly and obese. However, without knowing it, through a phone call they had begun to write their own chronicles of faith, love and service.

HARD TO CATCH

Long before he arrived at the Bible college, and while still in high school, Ralph was selected by his classmates as "Mr. Most Friendly." He has lived up to that reputation and prediction. This characteristic has been verified throughout his life. He is easy to get to know. He's a good guy! That made many of the girls at the college begin to take notice. Many considered him a good option as a potential boyfriend. But he disappointed them by not giving them special attention, but simply being friends with everyone.

Donna had a mentor who was instrumental in her training. She emphasized the importance of maintaining purity and taking a courtship seriously, so as to protect her good reputation as a Christian young lady and one very consecrated to the Lord. Donna began to recognize Ralph's intentions. He wanted to get to know her better and start a courtship. She, on the other hand, became the girl difficult to catch. Her concerned friends had told her, "Donna, you have to be careful; he has left a lot of girls hurt who thought they had a chance with him." Again, and again the warning was, "Be careful, he's going to break your heart." So, her strategy was to be cautious and make the way difficult. Donna took courtship very seriously and wanted to be sure that Ralph was the right one for her. However, Ralph's decision to court her became stronger and more intense.

LONG-TERM INTENTIONS!

As is often the case, the idea she had of Ralph before seeing him in person was different from when she finally met him. She spent a lot of time at the Bible college, even though she was in her last year of high school. At that point in the developing courtship, Donna liked Ralph very much, and Ralph realized that he was winning her heart. Typical in a growing relationship, he tried to find opportunities to be by her side and talk. Whatever the excuse, it was a unique opportunity to be close to her. He chose Valentine's Day as the time to, once and for all, let her know of his romantic intentions. He gave Donna a card and a gift. That marked the beginning of a slightly more serious courtship.

On June 9, after almost four months of dating, he formally and romantically asked her to be his wife. The next day he went to her house to ask her dad for her hand. When Ralph told him "I want to talk to you," Donna's father jokingly replied, "I think I should take a nap." However, he sat down, listened to him, and said, "Donna is very young, and she has just graduated from high school." "I'm not opposed," he added, "but take a little time."

Ralph's parents were impressed that their son had found a gal of Donna's caliber, who came from an excellent family.

They also gave their blessing and approval. Everything was set. They chose the date to get married a year after they got engaged. During their year of engagement, Ralph was in his second year of Bible college and Donna in her first. They were engaged on June 9, 1967, and married on June 8, 1968.

From the beginning of their courtship until they were married, they knew that the Lord was likely to use them in missions. They knew they were going to enter the ministry. They ministered together in duet at that time and one of the songs they sang said:

"Jesus, use me,
Lord, please don't refuse me.
Surely there is a work that I can do.
Even though it's humble,
Help my will to crumble.
Though the cost be great,
I'll work for you."

Those were the lyrics to the song they sang together even during courtship: " Help my will to crumble. Though the cost be great, I'll work for you." These words were more than just lyrics; it was the conviction of their heart.

The wedding planning was up to Donna. It was customary for the parents of the bride to bear the cost of the wedding. Thank goodness! In as much as Ralph was a Bible college student, he had very little to contribute to the cost of the wedding. The ceremony was wonderful, but somewhat long, lasting more than an hour with songs, poems, special music, and the participation of Donna's father and two other ministers who also officiated in the wedding.

PERPETUAL HONEYMOON

As a student at Bible college, Ralph didn't have much money to plan a significant honeymoon. They got married on Saturday nigh; Donna's cousin would be married on Monday, and Donna was to be in the wedding party. That meant they only had one honeymoon night. Ralph found a hotel that at that time was called Sweet Briar Inn. There they had the honeymoon suite that cost forty dollars. To book that dream suite, Ralph had to make a deposit and managed to make one of twenty dollars. On Saturday night, after the wedding, the new couple drove to the hotel that was forty minutes from the city. They got there and Ralph paid the remaining twenty dollars. They still have the receipt for that hotel; from what was the first night of hundreds and hundreds they have lived together.

The next day, on Sunday, they came back. Where? To the church! Yes, they were at the service that night. One of the pastors who had participated in the wedding was to preach in church that Sunday. When he saw them sitting there among the congregation, he said from the pulpit: "Look at this exemplary couple, they got married last night and today they are in the church service!" That Sunday afternoon, they had cleaned the apartment they were going to occupy at the Bible college, went to the rehearsal of the cousin's wedding and also to the church service in the evening. On Monday, they bought all the kitchen items and ran out of money. However, both went to work on Tuesday. About three weeks after they got married, they participated as counselors in a youth camp, and then began traveling throughout the United States, on behalf of the Bible college, to recruit new students.

How good God has been! He has rewarded them all these years allowing them to visit countless countries. They have stayed in many hotels and homes, enjoyed beautiful scenery, cruises and experiences of being in other nations. They have been exposed to many cultures and diversity. That has made them always say: *"Our honeymoon is not over yet. It's perpetual!"*

PART 3

FAMILY

STEPHEN BRENT

After leaving Bible college, Ralph and Donna were appointed pastoral assistants at a church in Detroit, Michigan. It was a ministry internship that was assigned in conjunction with the Bible college. It was a wonderful church. They moved to Detroit knowing that one day they would leave as missionaries. They were only there for a year and a half. But about seven months before leaving as missionaries, Donna became pregnant with their first child, Stephen Brent. They were headed to their assignment in the Caribbean and felt the urgency to expedite their departure from the states. They would live in San Juan, Puerto Rico. The plan was to get there in time for the baby to be born in beautiful Puerto Rico.

Married for three years and now seven months pregnant, they left Detroit, Michigan, for San Juan. They were very young. Ralph was twenty-three and Donna was only twenty-one. Upon arrival, they stayed in the house of the senior missionaries who had been on the island for years. They were an older couple who had never had children. The plan was to stay with them while looking for their own place with the hope of getting settled before the baby was born.

Only thirteen days after arriving in Puerto Rico, Donna's

water broke in the night. She needed to go to the hospital immediately. She woke Ralph up and told him to wake up the senior missionaries to take them to the hospital. At that time, they still had no house, no car, and the ship with all their household items had not yet arrived from the United States. They only had their travel luggage.

The missionary couple took them to the hospital around 2:00 in the morning. They were scared. They didn't understand much of what was happening because they had never had children, but they came to the hospital. Donna was immediately taken to the labor room; Ralph was left in a waiting room. The nurses did not speak English. Ralph and Donna didn't speak Spanish. No one understood anything and no one explained anything. The nurses talked to the missionary wife who understood very little, and of course, Ralph understood even less. At seven o'clock in the evening, almost seventeen hours later, Stephen was born. He was tiny, about 5 pounds. He had been born a month early. Being premature, he had to be in an incubator. In spite of these complications, Ralph and Donna were happy. Their first child had been born!

They learned a lot with the arrival of their first child and through the complication concerning his birth. It was a testing time. Perhaps, as a result of Stephen's early physical challenges, which he overcame, he would later easily adapt and confront challenges in missions with a heart to serve. Without a doubt, this is the key to his effectiveness in missions service. Thanks to Stephen, and his influence, many have joined the Mundo de Fe network, the fellowship of pastors led by the Hollands. Stephen's ability to encourage and lift others is the distinctive of his life. Without a doubt, he wears a unique mission mantle. Stephen has a very loving and tender heart, which allows him to quickly connect with people. He is quick to make sure that all are included in the activities so that no one misses out on God's blessing.

The length of your footsteps

Stephen accompanied his father on one of the trips to the

interior of the country in southern Costa Rica. He was about eleven years old at the time. To get to the church, they had to leave the pickup and walk on a path for about three miles, crossing several streams. They arrived at the small chapel just in time to enjoy a meal cooked over an open flame on a wood-burning stove and start the service.

At the end of the service, the church members returned to their small homes in the mountains while Stephen and Ralph laid down to sleep on the floor of the church building. However, at about two o'clock in the morning, one of the elders of the church woke them up. He insisted that they get up in a hurry and get out of there since the rains had begun to downpour up in the mountains and, consequently, the five small streams they would have to cross would soon become rivers with very strong currents.

Sure enough, they hurried and began to walk the three miles to where the truck had been left. Already the rain was falling on them and the dusty path had become muddy and slippery. They walked as fast as they could. They were on that trek when Ralph heard behind him the deep and agitated breaths of his son. He paused for a moment to ask if he was going too fast. Stephen responded with something that forever impacted Ralph's life: "Dad, it's not the speed of your walk, it's the length between your footsteps. I'm stepping in your footprints because I know it's firm and not slippery where you have walked." Incredible reflection from a son who desires to walk in the footsteps of his father! Ralph turned to continue walking, but now taking short, steady steps, weeping, and thanking God for the profound lesson God had given him through his son. You know, someone is following us; let's take firm steps for that someone.

Courtney

Courtney is Stephen's wife and has an inspiring life story of her own. She gave her heart to the Lord after finishing college. When she was starting her career —and still single— she felt and understood how difficult it is for someone who was not raised in the church to identify with the Christian community. That is why she wrote a book aimed at those who become Christians as young university students. The title is "Destined to Be." That book has impacted many lives!

The Lord also gave her a passion for the Muslim people. Precisely, at a time when Ralph and Donna were serving in a megachurch in Dallas, she organized an interest group for those desiring to reach Muslims. She studied much about the needs of the people, gave lectures and opportunities for guidance on how to reach them for Christ.

To Stephen and Courtney was born Ethan, who is the first male grandson for Ralph and Donna. It's amazing to see how he carries the same mantle and love for the Hispanic people and for missions. From a very young age, he has loved to travel with his father and even his grandfather. After having Ethan, Courtney went through a difficult battle with cancer. There was little hope of having another baby, but a short time later, their beautiful daughter, Madeline Emory, was born.

Winners do what losers do not want to do. They go to places that are not necessarily comfortable, and it is when they go to those places that they get stronger.

KAMELA MARIE

Two years after Stephen was born, while in the Caribbean, Kami, their daughter, was born. By that time Donna often felt like a "single mother" because Ralph traveled a lot from their Puerto Rican mission base. Every weekend he was in Haiti or in the Dominican Republic or starting the church in St Croix. Ralph founded a church in St. Croix and St. Maarten and visited other Caribbean islands. They lived in Puerto Rico for three years and eight months. Donna kept a record of her husband's travels, as he spent a third of his time outside of Puerto Rico working on the other islands. Donna could not accompany him on every trip in that she had two babies at the time.

During their time in Puerto Rico, Donna taught at the Bible school while investing time in learning Spanish. She would put her two babies in the car and go to the Bible school. While Donna taught the class, next to her in a small playpen, Stephen sat with his little sister. Yes, they were by their mom's side while she taught.

In 1973, she was born – as they call her – "our beautiful daughter Kamela Marie - Kami" on the island of Puerto Rico. She was a beautiful daughter and brought so much joy into their lives. She was the "middle" child. She was such a delightful child and was never a problem for her parents. On the contrary, she participated with them in missions and in the ministry. She spoke Spanish very well, embracing Hispanic culture with all her heart. She fell in love with and married Julio, a Cuban by birth, who had come to America as a very young child.

While still living in Dallas, they gave Ralph and Donna two beautiful granddaughters, Chelsea and Caroline. Chelsea was the first grandchild for Ralph and Donna and was actually born on Ralph's 50th birthday. Two years later, Caroline was born the day before Ralph's birthday. What a gift for Ralph and always a celebration at birthday time.

Later, life took them to Chicago and then to Denver, Colorado. Kami loved nature, the mountains and all the beauty of that place. She developed her own company of custom greeting cards, and she produced everything with great excellence and a touch of class. Among her clientele were many people of renown throughout the United States.

One day, Kami noticed that the mobility on her right side was not normal. She did not pay much attention since her dominant side was the left. But over time, the difficulty grew, and that concern led her to consult with a neurologist and, unfortunately, with an oncologist. After further examination, they gave her a hard, cold, and final diagnosis: brain tumor. Of course, for her parents the news was the hardest blow of their lives. But thanks to courage, faith, determination, always thinking about the positive and taking advice from doctors and the treatments they proposed, Kami was able to continue with her life for seven more years. It was a special time during which she was able to raise her daughters, who were sixteen and eighteen years old when she departed this life.

As Kami came to the end of her days, she wrote very significant words that contribute to this chronicle of pain and of victory. Knowing that the general diagnosis of her type of brain tumor was not favorable as far as recovery, but rather a progressive deterioration, Ralph and Donna's visits to Denver to be with Kami became more frequent.

On one such visit, shortly after Ralph and Donna arrived in Denver, the decision had to be made to take her to the emergency room. The headaches were intense, unbearable and the visit to the hospital was to get relief. They spent the next two nights with her in the hospital. It was on that occasion that Kami made the decision to suspend her treatments, as they would be more brutal and painful, but without any guarantee or promise of cure. They were with her and her husband at the time. There she made known her decision: "Enough is enough, I have fought a good battle, I am in God's hands, we will live what is left but no more treatments." There was virtually no hope with those procedures, and they would only inflict more pain and debilitation.

This decision caused Ralph and Donna to prepare to be in Denver for at least the next two weeks. They made a quick trip back to Dallas to resolve issues there that would free them for an extended time in Denver with their daughter. She was discharged from the hospital to spend her last days at home. Kami was now under hospice care and within two days slipped into a coma. On September 15, 2015, beautiful Kami, as her parents call her, went to be with the Lord. Her two brothers, Stephen and Tim, were able to spend precious time with her before her passing. Many friends from other states, and even other nations, joined her family to celebrate her life at a very beautiful funeral service.

Without a doubt, this was one of the most difficult trials for Ralph and Donna. The pain was simply unspeakable and indefinable. Only those who are parents of a child with a terminal diagnosis can truly understand the grief caused by the death of a child. Thank God the memories of who she was are simply wonderful. Her courage, the faith, and the hope with which she fought this battle was admirable. It is impossible to forget her words of encouragement in the face of adversity, her understanding of the meaning of life that she shared with many on her Facebook, and in opportunities to minister. She was able to impart this understanding in Spain and Nicaragua. These two conferences, given by her, were of enormous inspiration and blessing. She courageously recounted her experience of having to face uncertainty in this life while maintaining faith in the Lord. Her wisdom was simply admirable and abundant as many saw how she prepared her daughters to move forward and face life after she was gone. A difficult reality for her two precious daughters to face, but with grace and courage they have both excelled.

Finally, and as she told Donna, it was of the utmost importance to her that her experience with that tumor, in some way, served as a model, inspiration and legacy of encouragement for others in the difficult moments of life.

Deep Pain, Eternal Teaching

Psalm 34:18 took on a whole new significance to Ralph and Donna: *"The Lord is close to the brokenhearted; he rescues those whose spirits are crushed."* He doesn't take us out of the trials, he accompanies us through them. In difficult and painful times like these, we can't question "Where is God?", the answer is, "He is there, with us". Their hearts were broke, their spirits crushed, but the Lord was there. As deep as the pain was, deep and amazing was His love and companionship. One should not isolate themselves in pain and suffering. We need each other. We need support, faith, and encouragement that only God and others give.

Don't be afraid to embrace what you feel. In the process of grief, feelings collide. There are mixed emotions. On the one hand, you want to get on with your life; but, on the other hand, you think you will never be able to start over. It is when you realize that you must start again with your life that you enter that deep conflict that tells you that you must start and then sometimes that you should never start again. It is an unspeakable pain to want to reconcile the need to see, hear, touch, and embrace the loved one who has departed, and you are left with the harsh reality that you will never be able to do so again. There are pains that cannot be defined, and that is one of the greatest. When you still desperately want to see them again, talk to them, but you no longer can, you must start looking for ways to process and live with the new reality. At that point, the path of faith and hope that we have in God is not just another option, but is the best of all paths. That is precisely why Psalm 23 states, "He restores our soul." God does not remove the pain but offers the way for our life to be restored.

No one wants to live eternally with pain. In any case, we look for a way to be quickly free of it. But it is also true that emotional pain helps us to take it to the place where the Holy Spirit comforts us, helps us to overcome it. Pain makes us wonder: "How long will I have this suffering?" "Where is the solution?" In God, who restores the soul. Although we may not understand, it is not worth getting angry against God because He is not guilty. In any case, He is the restorer we need to rebuild life. He will be the best friend, the unconditional support.

Pain distracts you, prevents you from focusing on yourself and your need to embrace your future. Reading the Bible becomes difficult, especially when you almost know it by heart. But that is when there is only one thing left to do: decide to move on, keep getting up. **Relentless!** The hand of the Lord is outstretched to you – take it.

Pain can cause one to sleep too much or not sleep at all. Waking up unrested each day is indicative that you went to bed embracing the pain instead of the restoration. The same result happens with your appetite; you either eat a lot, or you do not want to try a bite. You do not feel entitled to eat when you remember that your loved one will no longer be able to eat. Different people react or respond differently to the processing their pain.

Therefore, for everyone, the advice is to cling to good memories. Take the time to remember the beautiful things that happened in life with the loved one who is no longer here. This helps to put aside the pain and add little by little to the final restoration.

Live from beautiful memories and do not let yourself sink in the pain of loss.

Loss is part of the human experience, it is inevitable, and it is also guaranteed, in a world that has not yet been completely redeemed and until we will live eternally with God. We must regain strength and move forward. That is what Kami would have said to her parents: "Mom, Dad, you've already cried too much, now move on with life!" So, allow yourself to feel the pain. You will receive healing. That will also connect you with the Holy Spirit so that you do not trust in your intellect or emotions, but in Him who will lead you to your best restoration.

Trust God. Hold on to memories. Let the pain heal.
Keep going.

TIMOTHY DAVID

Their third child, Timothy David "Tim" arrived! He came into the world in beautiful Costa Rica during the time when Ralph and Donna were serving there. He was always a very focused and responsible child. From a very young age, his musical talent was obvious. It was Miguel Cassina who identified Tim's gifting and mentored him in the ministry of praise and worship. That led Ralph and Donna to invite him to serve as worship pastor. Although, at first, he only mastered about three songs, his talent was evident. That is why Miguel insisted with Ralph to give him the opportunity. And the truth is that everyone was blessed when, at the age of fifteen, Tim, ushered the church into a spontaneous and profound ministry of praise. A true developing psalmist, such was his passion for music dedicated to God that he often went to the church at night to play the piano and spend long moments in worship before the Lord. A little later, they were given a piano, so the extended alone times in the church moved to the family home. Even after he was married, he had a small room, like a closet, where his piano was and became his place to worship the Lord. He has blessed the nations with the songs the Lord has given him.

On one occasion, he was given the opportunity to travel with a well-known group on weekends. At that time, he was studying at Christ for the Nations, a ministry school in south Dallas. After prayerful consideration, he opened his heart to Ralph, his father and pastor, about whether he should continue with those tours. "Tim," his dad told him, "Do what your heart feels, it's a good opportunity." However, Tim's response was surprising: "Dad, I feel that my first responsibility is with the local church, I do not want to miss every weekend. I want to dedicate myself to serving the Lord in Mundo de Fe."

What a decision! That choice is one of several indicators that signaled that he had the focus, strategy, and pastoral commitment to continue with the central church for the Mundo de Fe network of pastors and churches. Then the Lord gave him Abigail, his wife who, although not Latin, began studying Spanish while still in high school. In fact, she attended Mundo de Fe with a Hispanic friend to improve her Spanish, and it was there that she became better acquainted with Tim which subsequently led to their courtship and marriage.

Abigail

She was raised in a Christian home. Her parents served in the church as elders and then as care pastors in a megachurch. That certainly helped her understand how to embrace the people of the church; how to serve them more effectively in whatever they were going through. Her loving heart always keeps her focused on the needs of the family and personal needs of the people of the church. Her studies included a major in Communications, which would lead one to ask: "What can be done with a degree in Communications?" Knowing the power of language, how to use it and knowing how to write effectively and creatively, has given Abigail the tools to homeschool their five children. In addition, she has made good use of her time to write short thoughts of encouragement and exhortation in a very ingenious way through social networks and blogging. The creativity that the Lord has given her to share truths has been very interesting and impactful, as almost daily she ministers in this way to the believers and network connections.

Ralph and Donna are grateful to the Lord for giving Abigail as Tim's companion! A wife who, even before she met him, had a love for the Spanish language and for the Hispanic people. Of the five children they have –one son and four daughters – two have already graduated from Christ for the Nations Institute. After each of their graduations, Hannah and Susannah, intensified their involvement in ministry. Priscilla and Lydia are diligent students in their homeschool studies as they move toward their bright future. And the little boy, Timothy David II, even as a child, enjoys being in church and wants to be a part of every activity. So much so that he has already asked Tim when he will become the pastor! Thank God for the generational blessing He has given to Ralph and Donna.

PART 4

ON MISSION

Participation in missions is not sentimental philanthropy; it is just an honest man who pays his debt. This statement is based on Romans 1:14. "I have a duty to perform and a debt to pay both to Greeks and to barbarians (the cultured and the uncultured), both to the wise and to the foolish." -AMP- The debt we owe to humanity is the gospel.

– Warren Shibley

THE CALL OF GOD

Even prior to their marriage, Ralph and Donna were devoted to the Lord to serve in missions. As newlyweds, they lived on the campus of the Bible college while Ralph finished his ministry training. On one occasion, Ralph was out of a job and, although Donna was working part time in the office at the Bible college, they needed Ralph's income as well. At a college chapel service, with an emphasis on missions, the appeal was made for "faith promises" from students. This was the giving program to support foreign missions. Ralph took a faith promise card and committed to give fifty dollars monthly. The year was 1968. He, who was still out of work, showed the card to Donna. She replied that that sum was the same as what she was thinking. Thus, they turned in the card making a strong commitment, even though Ralph had no job.

At the end of that special mission service, moments before leaving the chapel, a fellow student who worked in a supermarket where Ralph had applied for a job, came running and said: "Ralph, my boss told me to tell you to please go to the store because it seems that he wants to offer you a job!" How excited Ralph was to see the answer to his faith promise come so soon! He immediately got in the car and left quickly for the supermarket. The boss offered him the job, even though Ralph had no experience in that chain of supermarkets. However, Ralph started at one of the highest salaries that the position afforded. Again, his boss told him: "I should not do this because you have no experience, and the labor union could question me. But something tells me that I have to give you the job this wage." That was a powerful lesson in acting by faith and commitment to the Lord. Ralph was blessed to work there until he finished college, and Ralph and Donna were able to faithfully give their monthly missions commitment. Trust God: He is faithful.

From Detroit to San Juan

After graduation, they moved to the city of Detroit, Michigan. The pastor of that church placed a lot of emphasis on missions. In another of those faith promise appeals, they again had to make a commitment of faith to which they responded with the sum of seventy-five dollars monthly. At that moment and looking into each other's eyes, Ralph said to Donna: "I think we are giving as much money as we can; the next step must be to give our lives to missions." This was the beginning of their journey to the mission field.

After a few months in Detroit, they attended a national convention where the custom was to dedicate Sunday afternoon to missions. When they entered the convention center to find seats, the Lord said to Donna, "Choose a seat where it will be easy for Ralph to go to the front when the call is made for those who want to commit their life to foreign missions." Donna chose the second seat and left the one on the aisle for Ralph. She somehow knew that the call to missions at that meeting would be very strong, even more so when they had their hearts beating hard for that area of involvement. Towards the end of the meeting, the call was made for those who wanted to dedicate their lives to missions. Donna knew that Ralph would run down to the altar. His response was immediate. He and Donna said "yes" to the call at that altar in August 1970.

Upon returning to Detroit, the pastor of the church, who had a heart inclined toward missions, began to support them in seeking God's will for the whole process and transition. The Mission Board learned of Ralph and Donna's commitment to become missionaries and offered them several opportunities that were open. They told them about the possibility of going to South Korea, but they knew this was not their destiny. But when they told them about missionaries who had served in the Caribbean needing an assistant, that opportunity caught their attention. They would reside in Puerto Rico as their base and from there assist in missions in Haiti, the Dominican Republic, the U. S Virgin Islands, and the British West Indies. It was a very challenging, but a very exciting opportunity. Their hearts were captivated.

The Holy Spirit confirmed that possibility and so they began with the preparations. Although Donna was pregnant with her first child, Stephen, they happily accepted this new and exciting opportunity. They would start by visiting churches, raising the support and monthly financial commitments to sustain them for the next four years. They did all of that very well and quickly. At the beginning of 1971 they were ready to go on location.

The only safe place is to have no other will, no other wisdom, but to follow the Lord wherever He takes you. Commitment must be perpetual.

-John Calvin

PUERTO RICO

Immediate obedience

The decision was to travel to the new destination on May 1, 1971. At this point, Donna was seven months pregnant. Many, especially women, asked them with concern: "If your child is going to be born in six weeks, why don't you wait here where you will be cared for by doctors from the United States?" Most everyone recommended, "Donna, plan to go to the mission field after your child is born." But she felt, even without knowing why, that they should not delay their departure and that the baby should be born in Puerto Rico. They flew from Detroit to San Juan, Puerto Rico, on May 1, 1971.

They arrived in the afternoon and immediately the missionaries who were waiting for them, took them to a meeting in the mountains of Puerto Rico. Without resting for a minute, they quickly left to attend that service. Ralph and Donna again showed that they are Relentless and that they are always ready for anything. Being ready for every opportunity has been their custom since the beginning of their ministry. In that mountain church, they had their first experience as missionaries, singing and participating in this unforgettable occasion. Definitely one of the secrets by which they have operated throughout their ministerial life has been that from the first moment both have blindly followed and obeyed the will of God. When they felt that He was calling them to serve, they did not come up with pretexts or excuses, or times or conditions. Responding immediately to God's commands was, and is, a hallmark in their lives. Certainly the Lord has honored that over the years.

Missions and a miracle

Ralph and Donna had no idea that Stephen would be born a month ahead of schedule. Confident that Donna still had more than a month of pregnancy ahead of her, Ralph and the supervising missionary made plans to go to St. Croix to start a new church. However, Stephen was born on Thursday night as they approached that weekend.

The missionary supervisor, instead of understanding that Ralph needed to be with Donna in the in the hospital, insisted on continuing with the plan for Ralph to travel with him to start the church. He thought that now that the baby was born, Donna could return home from the hospital without problems on the next Monday. However, on Friday afternoon the doctors advised them that they had detected a worrisome problem; Stephen was having difficulty swallowing. It could be due to an infection in his throat. The doctors expressed concern about the situation and continued with further testing.

On Sunday, the doctors felt that Stephen had improved and gave Ralph the release to travel to St Croix. However, within just a few hours, the doctor and a nurse gave Donna the result of all the studies that had been done. The news was harsh and indeed painful: "Mam, your baby was born without an esophagus." All the tests they did confirmed the diagnosis. These were not times with the modern equipment that is available today. However, they could detect the liquid he was given to swallow, including his own saliva, passed into his bronchi and lungs, so he had already developed pneumonia. His lungs were filling with everything he swallowed.

They made the decision to take Stephen to the University hospital, where a surgeon would make an opening in his throat to allow the saliva to drain continually and thus prevent it from going to go to his lungs. The plan was to insert a tube into his stomach, so that, using a syringe, he could be fed until he weighed at least 20 pounds; that is if the little guy survived the pneumonia he was suffering.

To proceed with all the suggested intervention on little Stephen required that Ralph sign all the necessary documents. Donna let hospital authorities know that her husband was on the island of St. Croix. At that time there were no cell phones, so the wife of the missionary supervisor helped Donna contact Ralph through the police in St Croix.

Ralph was in a meeting for the opening of the new church when the knock came on the door. The officer asked if Ralph Holland was present. When Ralph identified himself, the officer informed him of his need to return to Puerto Rico on the next available flight and proceed directly to the hospital. Emergency surgery was necessary, and as Stephen's father, he would have to sign a release for that to happen. Finally, and miraculously, Ralph managed to arrive and sign the papers for the operation.

Despite these complications, Stephen was a very cheerful baby who smiled a lot; few knew that underneath his clothing was a tube through which his mother fed him. At certain times the neck of his little shirt got very wet from the saliva that came out of the opening they had made in his throat to avoid liquid passing to his lungs.

A lot of people criticized Ralph and Donna telling them, "You should have waited for that baby to be born in the United States!" Some believed that they were out of the will of God to be in missions, and that was why they were going through this situation with their first-born child. The most painful thing was to hear, "Who knows if he's going to survive?" The comment was even made by a person in authority, "Don't cry; if he dies, you can have another baby."

The doctors had believed that after a year they would perform the corrective surgery on Stephen. But after ten months, he was so healthy he had reached the adequate weight to allow them to move forward with the procedure. The operation was complex and very risky for such a young baby. They would open him up through the abdomen to the back, collapse a lung and cut through the diaphragm. This would allow them to remove a piece of his large intestine and pass it through the diaphragm positioning it behind the lungs in the cavity where a normal esophagus is located. Although it would be a very complicated surgery, Ralph and Donna always felt that the Lord was with them, so they continued to trust Him with all their strength.

On one occasion, prior to the surgery, the tube through which they passed the food with a syringe became clogged, and they had to go quickly to the hospital. They managed to open it very quickly, but before leaving the hospital, the pediatrician who treated Stephen, introduced them to Dr. Pablo Rodríguez Millan. He was the only surgeon on the island of Puerto Rico who had ever successfully performed the surgery needed to correct Stephen's situation. He very patiently explained in detail the procedure that would need to be done. Ralph and Donna requested that he perform the surgery. He accepted their request and did the surgical intervention, which lasted almost 8 hours. It was a success, or rather, a huge miracle. They believe God allowed that tube to get clogged so that they could meet the surgeon on that visit to the emergency room.

Challenging requirements

When they arrived on the mission field in Puerto Rico, they assisted a senior missionary who was a former naval officer who was used to giving orders "military style." The senior missionary had been on location for several years prior to the arrival of Ralph and Donna. He and his wife had never had children. Perhaps that is why they did not understand the dynamics of a young family or understand the responsibility that entails. However, Ralph still respected him and did everything possible to serve him with honor, trying to exceed his expectations.

Ralph, who has often found himself working with strong

and somewhat demanding leaders, received from the Lord the grace to be gentlemanly, respectful, and submissive in those relationships. As well, he was determined to serve even a demanding missionary that was prone to shout at, and even humiliate, people under his authority. When Ralph returned from a trip to another island, the expectation was to check in with the senior missionary at his home to give a report and be assigned a new task, before ever going home to unpack and be with his family. The senior missionary measured everyone according to his own lifestyle. Since he claimed to never take a day off, he believed it was carnal and uncommitted to do so. Despite these and so many other details, Ralph's respectful and firm attitude made the relationship work with respect and honor. Perhaps the expectations of this supervisor contributed to the Relentless characteristic that has followed Ralph and Donna through ministry.

During almost four years of service in the Caribbean, Puerto Rico was the base and several surrounding island countries were the scope of their missionary assignment. Ralph was the one who had to travel with intensity and frequency, while Donna focused on the care of little Stephen and the pregnancy with Kami, the daughter who would be born in 1973. In addition to her family responsibilities, she was studying Spanish and teaching at the Bible school in Puerto Rico. In their years in Puerto Rico, Ralph logged an average of a flight every week to another island. Ralph and Donna were instrumental in founding five Bible training centers, mentoring leaders, and planting several churches. The memories of that experience are countless, the training was intense, and their commitment was affirmed.

Whatever the particular calling, the particular sacrifice God asks you to make, the particular cross He wants you to embrace, whatever particular path He wants you to follow, you will rise up and say in your heart, "Yes, Lord, I accept it, I submit, I surrender, I pledge to walk that path, follow that Voice, and entrust you with the consequences" Oh! but you say, "I don't know what he'll want next." None of us know! But we know that we will be safe in His hands.
-*Catherine Booth*

ST. CROIX

In a Bar on a Sunday

Although the vision was clear to open a church on the beautiful island of St. Croix U. S. Virgin Islands, finding a place to do so was a challenge. A location had not been determined. There was a bar that remained closed, and soon Ralph learned the history of the place and why it was closed. Every time someone opened that place, whether as a bar or restaurant, someone had been killed. Although the site had a bad reputation, Ralph rented it and there began the church in St. Croix. Although he later found another place, it was there that the church began offering services on Sunday mornings.

Many weeks he flew to St. Croix on Saturday and would sleep that night in a small room behind the platform in this bar transformed into a church. His temporary bed was the plywood floor. When the new believers realized that he was sleeping there, in a place where homicides had been perpetrated, they were afraid for him and suggested: "Come to our house. At least you can sleep on the sofa and be more comfortable and safer." That's how that beautiful church began. On a Sunday. In a bar.

It was in that beginning that Ralph had to return urgently to Puerto Rico to sign the documents to authorize the surgery within days of Stephen being born. Ralph continued to travel to St. Croix. Arriving on Saturdays, in the afternoon he would knock on doors inviting people to the church.

The first attendees to the new church were a very unchurched couple. Also in attendance was a woman who believed herself to be very spiritual; however, she was like the "woman at the well" that Jesus encountered. She lived with a man that was not her husband, but at the same time had a husband on another island. The three people that attended definitely needed an experience with God.

In that bar and nightclub that Ralph had rented to open the church, that couple who had offered Ralph their sofa on the weekends, immediately became believers. The transformation was beautiful. God began to work in their lives and Ralph began to disciple them. Soon other people started arriving and the church began to grow. A year after he began the church in St Croix, Ralph appointed that first convert, Lawrence, as the new pastor of the church. His work was an inspiration, he built a very solid and fast-growing congregation; and not only that, he also built one of the most beautiful church buildings on the island of St. Croix. Ralph and Donna still maintain contact with him.

Lawrence became a very faithful tither; he earned good money as a skilled finished carpenter. He could build anything. The first pulpit Ralph used to preach in St. Croix was a result of his craftsmanship. The second Sunday in the new location, Ralph heard a commotion outside the building and realized that Lawrence, the new convert, had arrived with the pulpit he had made.

A very humorous anecdote took place between Ralph and Lawrence, but it did show the tight friendship. As God blessed him, and as he prospered, he was able to buy a property in a new development in the center of the island. It was an upscale and desirable urban development. He invited Ralph to go to the property to dedicate it to the

Lord. Ralph was honored to do so. Ralph arrived at the property which consisted of two very large adjoining lots. While there, Ralph asked him: "Where is the center of the property?" In response, he took him to the very center of the combined lots. Standing there, Ralph prayed the dedicatory prayer and then jokingly added: "You are a good tither, so ten percent of this property belongs to me, and I want my ten percent right here in the center." But Lawrence didn't understand it was in jest so very seriously he responded: "Pastor, I'm going to have to change my construction plans, because the house I'm going to build will occupy some of that section in the center, so I'm going to have to revisit the architect." Then Ralph burst into laughter and told him it was in jest, which was a relief to the dear brother.

He was, without a doubt, a sincere, obedient, submissive, docile man willing to submit to whatever was expected of him. Why? . . . because he wanted to serve the Lord in everything and with everything. For that reason, the Lord used him greatly. Today his son is the pastor and the church on the island of St. Croix continues to move forward.

While Ralph traveled every weekend to different islands to start a new church or minister in the established churches, Donna learned to take advantage of these times while she remained behind with their two small children. A much-loved mentor, told her something very wise concerning the life of the missionary wives and mothers who often had to stay at home and spend a lot of time raising the children without their husband present: "Recognize that this is a very unique phase in your family dynamic, and these will not necessarily be the best years of your life." By explanation of this statement, and not to be misunderstood, it came from her understanding of the reality that came with the responsibility of raising children in unusual circumstances unique to missionary life. Donna began to take advantage of those times of forced solitude at home to study and prepare for the day she would work with more prominence in the ministry. She did not want to waste time, so she made it a priority to make the most of learning and improving her Spanish, to enrich her life with the Word of God and with many books and many studies that were part of her formation in ministry. In that she couldn't travel, she strived to make good use of her time.

Occasionally, Donna was able to accompany Ralph. On other occasions, they traveled as a family, although not as many times as they would have liked. The budget and conditions on arrival were often not adequate for a family with small children. When they eventually moved to Costa Rica, they would go out together to serve different parts of the country by land transportation, be it public buses or their own vehicle.

On one occasion when Ralph returned from a trip, he immediately noticed that Stephen resented that his dad was gone so much. Ralph was scheduled to make another trip the very next day. Seeing Stephen's reaction, Ralph asked Donna to pack a suitcase for Stephen as well. That day he traveled with his two-year-old son! People looked at them with questioning stares as it was unusual to see a dad who was traveling alone with such a young son. But it was impossible for Ralph to leave his little boy once again.

I have nothing to offer but blood, work, sweat and tears.
- Churchill

HAITÍ

Mosquito nets and diapers

Stephen was twenty-one months old, and Donna was seven months pregnant with Kami. Donna was scheduled to teach in the Bible school in Haiti. This meant that she and Stephen would join Ralph on the flight to Port-au-Prince. This time they would not stay in a hotel, but in the house of a Haitian pastor. He had a comfortable house by Haitian standards, considering that the country was the poorest in the entire Western Hemisphere. They had to sleep under mosquito nets. Among the shortcomings, the most notorious was the lack of a traditional indoor bathroom. A makeshift outhouse was attached to the house. To use this outhouse was an interesting ordeal. First, they had to send the cockroaches running.

To economize, they hardly ever used disposable diapers for Stephen; he used cloth diapers because of the advantage of washing and reusing them. But, when they traveled, for a matter of convenience and comfort, they used disposable diapers. They were not available in Haiti so one piece of luggage contained disposable diapers. A Haitian lady who cared for Stephen while Donna taught, didn't know how to use those disposable diapers.

When Donna returned from class, she found that the caregiver had attempted to wash the disposable diapers. There was no cotton left in the diaper! It was a hilarious sight to see the outer plastic of disposable diapers hanging on the clothesline with a few remaining strands of the fiber lining hanging down!

The poverty level in Haiti is indescribable. Every time Kami moved inside Donna's womb, she prayed, "Please Lord, don't let me go into labor. I don't want my baby to be born here. Let me get back to Puerto Rico for her birth." How challenging this part of the missionary work was. But, it was a special experience that was marked in her mind as part of her unconditional service to the Lord.

Heat and a white shirt

As was the case most of the time, the heat was overwhelming and air conditioning was non-existent. The tropical heat was simply unbearable. The churches were filled to capacity with worshippers. In the churches there were no nurseries or children's ministry where they could leave Stephen. So, between the two of them they had to share childcare. Sometimes Donna played the accordion for the worship, so Ralph took care of Stephen. On one occasion, Ralph had to take care of Stephen while he preached.

Yes, he had the little guy in his arms on the platform. It is worth remembering that the supervising missionary did not allow him to go dressed down for the heat. He had to wear a suit, white shirt, and tie, even with the suffocating heat. But Stephen knew nothing of those rules. Stephen became overheated, got sick and vomited on his father. He filled Ralph's suit with vomit, even filling the pockets of the jacket! All that happened on the platform and in plain sight. As there was no place to cleanup, Ralph just passed Stephen off to Donna and went to the pulpit to preach with a very unpleasant smell, but the assignment was completed!

It was customary for them to include their young children in their missionary activities. So, while Donna played the accordion for the worship services, she sat them next to her in a baby carrier. First it was Stephen, then Kami, and finally Tim. The children were always there, next to Donna at the meetings. They did not have the luxury of a nursery, nor a place to take care of children. Throughout the experience of raising their children on the mission field, they learned to be in the meeting, sit still, and behave well while Mom and Dad went about ministry.

The Jeep and the truck

In Haiti, Creole is spoken, and Ralph learned some basic expressions to be able to communicate. He was just learning Spanish as well, but he had a good understanding of French. But not only was the language a challenge, so were hundreds of anecdotes that made his work in Haiti an unforgettable assignment.

Ralph, Donna and little Stephen, along with the supervising missionary, experienced a true miracle. They had a 1959 "Willys" Jeep. It was an old open vehicle with a canvas top. They traveled all over the country in this old vehicle. On one occasion, with little Stephen along with them, they made a trip to the interior of the country. They were on their way to a very remote area together with the missionary and the translator. The senior missionary was at the wheel, with the translator at his side. Donna and Ralph with Stephen in Ralph's arms were sitting on a small and insecure bench seat. They were moving along on one of the few straight roads in the country. Suddenly, a truck loaded with wood crossed the road in front of them without time to avoid an accident. The missionary tried to slow down and avoid the accident, but it was impossible. The Jeep went up under the truck and the fragile structure that supported the canvas that served as the roof was destroyed. The frame that held the canvas bent and ended up brushing the top of Ralph's head while he protected Stephen with his embrace. If the frame had bent an inch more, the story would be different as the weight of the truck dragged the Jeep into a small river, but miraculously stopped before crushing them underneath. They were quickly able to get out; they were not injured, but very scared. A miracle. The

Jeep was embedded under the truck; however, they were safe and sound.

At the crash site, they sat on the side of the road. The people of the nearby countryside began to realize what had happened. Although no houses could be seen anywhere around, people began to come from everywhere. They came running to confirm that there were no injuries. A lady, to express her concern, came with an old aluminum cup full of water. It was very polluted water from the river or some well. Since it was not drinkable, despite their great thirst, they chose not to drink it. That woman also offered water to Stephen. Those wonderful people offered the best they had.

Finally, a vehicle arrived that took them to Port-au-Prince, the capital of the country. The next day, they returned to the crash site to see how to get the Jeep out with a wrecker and take it to the city to fix it so it would be ready for future trips!

Unforgettable baptisms

In Haiti, they customarily organized many conferences with thousands of people in attendance. And the number of baptisms that took place was very significant. In the large auditorium they had built, they included a baptistry. On one occasion, a lady was so moved by her baptism that when Ralph lifted her from the water, she made a single leap from the baptistry to the floor shouting as she rejoiced in the presence of the Holy Spirit. That was an amazing experience, but not unusual to witness the joy that only God can provide in their humble lives.

On another occasion, Ralph and Donna traveled to the interior of the country. There they were to baptize believers from a church that met in a facility made of bamboo and thatch. They had the meeting, and then they all went to the river to start the baptisms. The river was not deep, perhaps only a depth of about two feet of water. They had to dig to achieve greater depth and thus be able to submerge people more easily. To baptize, Ralph would sit them on the riverbed and then submerge them. That he did with fifty-two people! Many times, when he placed his hand on the heads of those who were baptized, he noticed that they were burning with the high fevers. The need was extreme, and illness was commonplace.

After the baptisms, they took Ralph to the "pastoral house," a humble one-room hut with a dirt floor and thatched roof. The kitchen was outside in the courtyard because they cooked with firewood. So, Ralph went in the hut totally wet to change his clothes. He was in that process when the pastor's wife entered the hut. Ralph was standing there with his wet clothes now on the dirt floor, about to have a heart attack due to embarrassment. To make matters worse, there was no other room or piece of furniture to jump behind to cover himself. She had brought in the basin of water for "the pastor to bathe." The situation was normal for her, she had no shame nor was it embarrassing to see Ralph that way. So, she calmly said: "Water pastor," or "L'eau pastor" in French, to which Ralph replied in desperation "oui, oui!" She then gave Ralph the basin and left the hut as if nothing had happened. At that time in Haiti – decade of the 70's – nudity was very common. They bathed in the rivers and walked around their own homes without the decency that we would expect. Part of the pastoral task was to teach people to be modest.

Haiti's extreme poverty is difficult to comprehend! It always amazes one to see the simplicity and misery of its people, but it also amazes one to see what the Lord Jesus Christ can do with them and among them. The need is so great; to this day, the challenge still exists throughout the country.

Land Cruiser and a nut and a bolt

Eventually, they were able to exchange the old and worn-out Jeep for a much better one. Now they had a Jeep Land Cruiser. They found themselves once again crossing the mountain to go to the other side of the island. The road was in very bad condition, which made the car vibrate and bounce around too much. The vibration was so strong that a nut was shaken loose from the transmission differential, causing the drive shaft to fall to the ground. That happened a long way from mechanical help. The question was obvious: "What do we do now?" They were far from the city and in the middle of the mountain... so, how to fix the serious damage if there is no mechanic nearby to do it?

The best Ralph could do was pray. He walked up and down next to the Jeep praying "Lord, what do we do?" Few cars passed by; maybe just one per day. On his prayer walk, Ralph, now behind the vehicle and still praying, noticed that laying amongst the rocks was the nut that had fallen off. He crawled under the Jeep and put the nut back by hand and adjusted it as much as he could. They got back on the road and reached their destination without any further problems. Once again, they will always believe there was divine intervention that allowed that little piece to fall within view of a praying Ralph!

One night in the Jeep

Among so many experiences, there is also one more unforgettable incident when they crossed the mountain, again in the old Willys Jeep. Near the top of the mountain, the Jeep stopped and would not restart. It seemed like perhaps they had run out of gas. However, there was plenty of gas in the tank. But, for some reason, it did not start. Not at all. It was already sunset, and there was no way it would start. And, because it was at the top of the mountain, and getting dark, no one passed by. The "road" was just a path for people to walk; it was not really intended to be used by vehicles. But that path was the only way they could reach the destination. Nighttime approached and darkness set in. Although Haiti is very hot during the day, in the mountains the cold is quite extreme at night, and they did not have adequate clothes for that climate. To cope with the cold weather, Ralph had an idea. He removed the large hood and placed it on the side of the Jeep, which had no doors and was open. In this way he shielded the wind from hitting them so forcefully. There they remained until sunrise, sleeping in the Jeep.

At dawn the next day, a gentleman walked up. He was a very poor man who lived in the bush. It was evident that he was from a hut around there. He asked them what had happened. The translator was sitting in the Jeep. He proceeded to tell him the details of the incident. The humble farmer said, "Try to start it," but the Jeep did not respond. So, he disappeared into the bush for about an hour. He then returned with a screwdriver and a piece of copper wire and got under the Jeep. He removed the gas pump, the diaphragm, and that little "arm" on the gas pump that is like a small finger that pumps the gasoline. It was totally worn out and so it no longer worked! He wrapped the piece of copper wire around the arm on the pump as many times as it would go around, mashing it tightly on the pump piece until it was built up where it would make contact with the pump diaphragm and pump the gasoline. Then he said, "Now try it again." They turned the ignition and soon it started up! They were able to finish their missionary journey and return to Port-au-Prince, with a gas pump fixed with wire by an unknown Haitian after having spent a night in that beloved Jeep. That man, who came from who knows where and with what was needed to fix the Jeep, may well have been an angel!

Ralph and Donna spent four years in missions work in Haiti. It was a wonderful experience and time of training for the future. They baptized hundreds of people throughout the country. They planted about a hundred churches and built many small church buildings with capacity for eighty to a hundred people. Ralph and the supervising missionary always worked together in the construction of those chapels. A large facility, known as "The Tabernacle," was built in Port-au-Prince. The work was great, the needs were greater, but the Lord is greater than all of them, so the mission was possible.

> "This is no time for peace and comfort. It's time
> to dare and endure."
> — *Churchill*

SINT MAARTEN

Ralph had already opened the church in St. Croix. Nearby is another island –Sint Maarten – half French and half Dutch. Thanks to some contacts he had there, he and the supervising missionary decided to open a church on the island. Ralph, by that time, was twenty-five years old. Upon arrival on the island, he would rent a small motorcycle which is a common mode of transportation by the islanders. The island was not as touristy at that time as it is now.

Ralph set out to travel the entire island, looking for a place that met the most basic conditions to begin to gather people and open a church. On the middle of the island, he found a field with a humble abandoned cement building standing among the overgrown weeds. He decided to ask the owner if he could arrange to rent that building to use as a church. The owner began to laugh, which surprised Ralph, until the owner explained the reason for his laugh: "Well, this building is a pigsty, a pigpen." There they kept the pigs; there they ate, slept, and did their physiological needs. But the owner responded in the positive: "If you want to clean it, then well, you can use it."

What did Ralph do? He bought everything he needed to

clean and prepare that deplorable place, including a shovel with which he took out all the excrement. They then began with the operation of "cleaning the most unclean pigsty that has ever been seen." This included washing the walls. When they finished, the place was very presentable. It could now be said that there was a church in the pigsty. The wonderful thing was not an empty pigsty, but rather another place of worship where people gathered!

With time, Ralph trained a pastor from that region for the growing congregation. The fulfilling reward for his sacrifice came after almost forty years when Ralph and Donna visited that island. The congregation had built a two-story facility, about a hundred yards from where the pigsty still stood. Ralph was curious to know what had finally happened to that kind man who had allowed him to open the church there.

It was a Sunday and service was being conducted in their beautiful building. Ralph approached the building to look inside. Ralph got the attention of an usher standing near the door and began asking him questions about the history of the church and how they had come to build it. The usher looked curiously at him and asked, "Are you Ralph Holland?" "Yes, I am," he said, "I founded this church about forty years ago." The usher was so happy to see Pastor Ralph and explained: "Well, here they do not stop talking about you and the impact you were in the beginning!" He also told him that the owner of the pigsty had died, but that his son said that all his life, until his death, his father spoke of the kind American who came to establish that church in such a humble place. "But look now," the usher concluded excitedly, "It has come to be a beautiful two-story, crowded church building." Glory to God for another humble beginning, but with miraculous results.

"Life is a daring adventure or it's nothing."
- Helen Keller

DOMINICAN REPUBLIC

With the same passion with which they served Haiti, Ralph and Donna served in the Dominican Republic. The two countries share the large island of Hispaniola. It was there that Ralph preached his first message in Spanish. His expectations regarding the results of that first message were very idealistic. He thought that his sermon was going to last who knows how long, that it was going to be powerful, strong, and that everyone was going to be impacted by it. But it only lasted nine minutes. He preached and sat down. He had used all the Spanish that he knew to express his thought.

From Santo Domingo, they would travel to the interior of the country towards the border with Haiti. Because of the proximity, many Haitians worked on the farms in the Dominican Republic, forming Haitian communities within the country. Ralph and Donna ministered there often carrying the gospel. They established several churches in these communities. They had to tolerate unbearable heat, without the blessing of air conditioning and with countless limitations. During one of those visits, Stephen became very ill with diarrhea. What to do to prevent dehydration?

One of the interesting tips to prevent risks to the health of their children was suggested by their pediatrician. He recommended that they periodically give them a little of the well-known Coca-Cola. The doctor explained that it was the best quick remedy when they suffered from diarrhea because Coke replenishes the electrolytes in the digestive system. On many occasions, there was no other option than to drink Coca Cola when traveling through the interior of the Dominican Republic or Haiti. Tap water could not be consumed and getting bottled water was simply impossible. Maybe that's why today Stephen continues to drink "too many" Cokes.

The hotel they stayed in during the first years of their travels to Santo Domingo is still unforgettable. It was called Hotel Colón. Such was the condition of the hotel, that Ralph and Donna joked: "Surely Columbus (Colon is the Spanish word for Columbus) must have stayed here when he discovered the Americas." It was a run-down hotel, dirty and without any appeal or comfort. But that is where they stayed. It was common to use mosquito nets, one and another ceiling fan, without air conditioning, with the windows always open and with a bathroom that made the experience something not to talk about.

But later they found another hotel, a little more comfortable, called Hotel Victoria. "If Columbus had stayed at the previous hotel, Queen Victoria must have stayed in this one!" joked Ralph and Donna. Of course, those hotels were nothing like the amazing hotels that exist today in the Dominican Republic. But in those times that was the only option because tourism had not been developed. Anyway, the condition of the hotels was a simple detail that did not deter them from doing the will of God and reaching this nation with the gospel.

Creative Architecture

The scope of work during the years in the Caribbean included a lot of assignments in the Dominican Republic. Ralph and Donna have ministered to every socioeconomic level throughout their lives. In Santo Domingo, there is a neighborhood called "Los Guandules", one of the poorest and most conflictive "barrios" in the city, a place where many gangs based their operation. A wonderful lady pastor had a congregation that met in a shack made of leftover pieces of lumber, a roof made from a few sheets of tin, and it had a dirt floor. Seeing that congregation's need, Ralph and Donna raised funds to build a block building with a concrete floor.

Ralph determined to build this church in just ten days. He hired some masons and laborers to help him and began the process of building the new house for the Lord. To build quickly in the time Ralph had allotted, he assigned a block layer to each side of the building. They worked from sunrise until sunset. Even Ralph worked alongside those with the task of laying blocks. When the walls reached the projected height, it was time to place the beams, the rafters, and the new tin roof. Ralph built the beams and rafters, and then they hoisted them to the top of the walls and the tin roof was nailed to the rafters. After finishing the structure, they painted it.

They were proudly satisfied to have managed to build the building, and even paint it, in just ten days. Ralph went out to the street to take a picture of this miraculous ten-day construction project. But when he focused the camera, he noticed something odd. What a shock! The right wall was at least six inches higher than the left wall -- which resulted in a roof "tilted" to the side. It was certainly an unusual architectural design. The result? A happy pastor, an impressed congregation, the best building in the entire community built in ten days, and a new place for God's presence.

Mistaken identity

Ralph, in his mid-twenties, traveled very frequently to the Dominican Republic. At that time, they flew with cheap tickets because the airlines gave significant discounts to missionaries. On one of Ralph's arrivals at the Santo

Domingo airport, he had an unusual experience. While standing in line, an airline agent came running to take his documents and told him he didn't have to stand in line, and that he would take care of everything. He explained that he was going to process all of the documentation for him through immigration and claim his luggage. Ralph was very surprised.

Why this special treatment? Of course, Ralph enjoyed the attention. After having ministered in Santo Domingo, he returned to the airport and at the airline counter, the same agent appeared again and said: "You are not going to stand in line; give me your passport, and I will process your documents and check your luggage. You go to the VIP lounge to wait, and I will see you there." When it was time for the flight to board, the agent came for Ralph and took him to a first-class seat on the plane, even though he had bought a very cheap ticket. Every time he arrived in Santo Domingo, he received the same treatment. Immigration, baggage claim, VIP lounge and first class.

On another trip, Ralph was chatting with a fellow passenger who offered to share the taxi fare from the airport to Santo Domingo. It was a rather long ride, and the taxi was somewhat expensive. Ralph accepted the offer and said: "That's a deal, but just so you know, I will be waiting for you outside. When I arrive, I will not have to stand in line." Sure enough, once again the agent came running and gave Ralph the royal treatment. He was ushered through immigration and customs and waited for his taxi companion outside.

When they both got into the taxi and started their journey into the city, his travel companion said, "I see that they treat you very well here in the Dominican Republic." Ralph replied yes, but that he did not know why they always treated him so special. The new acquaintance said, "I know why." "Why?" Ralph asked. The man replied, "Because you look exactly like the U.S. ambassador here in the Dominican Republic. You look identical." "Anyone could mistake you for the Ambassador!" That explained it all! Ralph told himself that he needed to let the agent know that he was not the ambassador and that surely that preferential treatment would no longer be offered to him.

When he arrived back at the airport, the agent again came running to help him. Ralph quickly said, "Sir, just a moment please, I am not who you think I am." Then the agent lowered his head and replied, "Yes, I know. I realized that several trips ago, but I couldn't figure out how to stop the preferential treatment I had given you." Then Ralph replied, "Well, that's okay, you can just keep it up. I am an ambassador in the Kingdom of God."

A Passion for the Dominican Republic

After their four years in Puerto Rico and traveling to the islands, they had agreed with their mission board that for the next four years, they would concentrate in the Dominican Republic exclusively. However, a change in plans took place, and Ralph and Donna went to Costa Rica. Ralph and Donna had their heart set on serving in the Dominican Republic. Yes, more than they had already done while based in Puerto Rico. Much later, even after arriving in Dallas, and during their time as pastors of Mundo de Fe, that passion remained.

A Dominican pastor, serving in Playa del Carmen, Mexico, became part of the Mundo de Fe network. He shared the same great desire with Ralph to have representation of the network in his country, although he lived in Playa del Carmen. They agreed to go together for a weekend to do an evangelistic outreach to see what would happen.

Without them knowing it, the Lord was already calling a couple to go and serve like Abraham, who had gone to a country, based on the urging of the Holy Spirit, without knowing what they were going for. They had already sold everything they owned and were on location in the Dominican Republic. Ralph coincidentally learned that this couple, with a history with Mundo de Fe, had already moved to the Dominican Republic and invited them to be part of that outreach. They agreed and joined the outreach.

Their spirit connected with the passion, and they accepted the invitation to continue with the people that were converted as a result of that crusade. The decision was quickly made for them to become the missionaries for Mundo de Fe in the Dominican Republic.

They have established a church in Santo Domingo and networked with other ministries, doing an excellent work in that country. An interesting note is that the building they rented as a church happened to be located on "Costa Rica" Street. Incredible! Years earlier, Ralph and Donna had submitted to their oversight, and had gone to Costa Rica instead of Dominican Republic. Later, in Santo Domingo, the church was established on a street named "Costa Rica." It's like the Lord smiled a bit at them saying *look how, I have everything well connected in the trajectory of your life!*

COSTA RICA

As they approached the end of their time as missionaries in Puerto Rico, the mission board encouraged Ralph and Donna to think about serving in another country, such as the Dominican Republic or Haiti. The desire was to go to the Dominican Republic. They proceeded to find places to live in coordination with the location of the American school in English, ideal for Stephen to start his schooling. They were sure that their new home would be in the Dominican Republic. But one night, the mission board met to discuss the plan and interrupted their sleep for the rest of the night with a phone call that meant another time of seeking a confirmation from God. Ralph and Donna agreed to prayerfully consider the suggestion by the board to serve in another country.

The suggestion was that they consider opening a new country for their denomination – the beautiful country of Costa Rica. There was no mission of the denomination in that country, and they wanted to establish a mission base there. At that time, they were sending missionaries to El Salvador, Panama, and Honduras. The message from the board was, "We want you to consider Costa Rica." That suggestion took Ralph and Donna by surprise. Their thought was, "We are so young, and they entrust us to open a completely new mission field!" They felt inadequate to the task, but the board did not stop insisting. There was a Spanish language school in Costa Rica that hundreds of missionaries would attend each year on their way to their mission destination. The board wanted to route their missionaries through this school, and Ralph and Donna become the ones to receive them.

So, once again, Ralph and Donna immersed themselves in prayer. The Lord gave His confirmation for them to accept the challenge of opening the mission in Costa Rica. First, they took a short trip to see how they felt in the new land. They didn't know anyone. They rented a car and explored the country as much as possible, mainly San José, its capital. At that time Costa Rica was an extremely peaceful country, known as the "Switzerland of Central America." It was a beautiful place to live, but as always, their focus was missions.

When they left the United States for Costa Rica, it was to begin a life by faith. Not so much in terms of finances, because they had already reached the budget with the necessary commitments to supply the funds, but because they were going with two small children and little knowledge of what the new challenge would entail. Ralph was twenty-eight years old; Donna, twenty-six; Stephen was four and Kami was two. They were going to a place where they had never lived and did not know anyone.

When they arrived, they stayed in an extended stay facility for a few days until they found a house, bought furniture, and waited for the arrival of their personal effects to establish their home. Donna openly admits that at that point she was very dependent on her husband's faith. She has always been a wife willing to walk by his side and support him. But she wasn't as extroverted and ready to take on a new challenge nor as adventurous as he was.

They found a comfortable house in a very nice neighborhood, got a car, and Ralph began to drive all over San Jose praying and asking the Lord to guide him to the perfect location to start the work. One day, in "Desamparados," a section of

San Jose, he felt very strongly that it was of the Lord to start in that location. He found a corner lot that was empty and next to it were two wooden houses for rent. The location was ideal being on a main bus route and busy street. So, on that empty lot he decided to put up some lights and a platform with a provisional roof. That's how they started, under the stars on a vacant lot.

They had become acquainted with believers of similar faith and vision. These new friends showed up to support the new endeavor. A missionary friend from Nicaragua also came to support them. He sang and preached in Spanish. There were several conversions, and many were baptized at the close of that crusade. Ralph rented those two wooden houses next to the empty lot and there began the church. That location would later become the central church in Costa Rica.

The wounded side

When they were building the first building in the location of the original wooden houses, a near tragedy happened. A brother who became a church leader and was a builder was leading the construction. One day, he was there at work and the blocks were stacked and waiting to be laid. The foundation had already been laid, the beams were in place and the rebar was set in concrete.

At one point, the builder heard someone talking or calling outside. To look out and determine who it was, he peeked over the blocks and lost his balance. When he fell, one of the iron rods (rebar) pierced his side and damaged a rib. In fact, it penetrated from just under his ribs, through his chest and came out near his neck, passing through the area of his collarbone. He was unable to free himself from the rebar. He began calling for help. When Ralph heard him, he ran desperately towards him. He was a rather heavy man, but that didn't stop Ralph from lifting him slowly off the rebar until he was totally freed.

When Ralph got him off the rebar, he wanted to put him

in the car and take him quickly to the hospital, but he replied: "I'm going to be fine, don't worry, I'll be fine." Ralph insisted: "No sir, that's a construction rod that has gone through your body. You have to go to the doctor now." Finally, he was taken to the hospital and was immediately examined, they did X-rays and cleaned the entire area where the iron had passed through his body. Stitches were done on his injured side and neck, and he returned home to rest.

But to Ralph's surprise, the next day, when he should have been resting, he showed up to work. There he was at 7:00AM in the construction of the church building once again. Ralph tried to convince him to return home. But the brother refused and continued to work as if nothing had happened. In less than a day, he felt he had recovered from the accident and was determined to continue, despite the pain, until finishing the construction. He was a great man of faith and commitment, visibly demonstrated by his response to what could have been a life-threatening tragedy. He was there until he finished his work and was one of the most outstanding members of the new congregation. What an inspiration!

The church began to grow. Several young people in those early days were converted, and Ralph and Donna found themselves needing to start a Bible school. There was no ideal place to do that, so it began in their garage. There they set up desks and began to teach every night and train around twenty young people. They became part of the family. Many times, Donna had to prepare food for everyone. Rice, beans and sometimes meat with some sauce.

At that time, Donna understood what it was like to have her house open, to attend to people, to receive them with open arms as they all diligently studied the Word of God. The church was young; and so were Ralph and Donna. Most of their converts were people between the ages of nineteen and twenty-nine. This made them become a very close group. Many of them who were trained there, left San Jose, and started churches throughout the country.

During the course of time in Costa Rica, Ralph and Donna planted seventeen churches, including a very strong central church with a beautiful facility with an auditorium to accommodate seven hundred people and a Bible school facility. God honored their dedication, and they give Him all the glory!!

Ralph and Donna strongly believe that if someone considers themselves to be a missionary, they should devote their entire lives to ministry and missions, even if there is no one around supervising them and calling them to accountability. It was important for them to get up every morning and have a plan to extend the Kingdom of God; to go to visit a church, to teach at the Bible school, to evangelize, to take advantage of each day. This ethic has always been their way of serving and fulfilling their calling.

Asleep in a service . . .

Ralph was to go to the mountain to preach in a church where he had helped them build a little wooden building. They had to drive five hours in the pickup truck and then continue the journey on horseback for three more hours until they reached the community.
It was a small church building made of wood cut with a chainsaw. That was a very laborious endeavor. To make planks from the logs, they built a frame and mounted the chain saw. Then they passed the logs over the frame and by the mounted chainsaw producing rustic planks.

Ralph took a missionary, who was in Costa Rica studying Spanish, with him on this particular trip. Ralph and the guest missionary arrived at the church on the mountain after dark. Upon arrival, they were greeted with a special meal cooked with firewood. The kitchen with the wood-burning stove was connected to the church auditorium. As a result, the entire church was filled with smoke. Before the meeting began, Ralph was already well exhausted and overcome by the smoke. In addition to the smoke from cooking, the lanterns used for light burned a type of crude oil that generates a smoke that makes the eyes burn.

As they gathered in the church to begin the service, Ralph and the men of the congregation stood leaning against the wall. There were no benches or chairs, just some wooden logs that had been cut in the forest. Women sat on the logs and the men stood around the outer wall. Around fifty people had assembled for the service. They sang and testified, and Ralph, tired from the trip and the smoke, fell asleep on his feet.

The missionary who was standing next to him, since he did not yet understand Spanish well, did not understand everything the pastor was saying. At one point in the service, the pastor said something and mentioned Pastor Ralph Holland. But Ralph was still standing in his sleep and heard nothing the pastor said. The missionary accompanying him thought they were calling Ralph to preach and gave him a nudge with his elbow to wake him up. "Pastor Ralph, I think they just introduced you to preach," he said. Ralph woke up, went straight to the pulpit, and began preaching. To this day, Ralph does not know if they introduced him to preach or were only acknowledging him as a guest in the service that night. But nevertheless, Ralph went to the pulpit, preached his message, and closed the meeting.

There's a pig in my car

Ralph and Donna loved to include as many as they could in their travels to the other cities and towns of Costa Rica to provide encouragement for the growing body of believers throughout the country. All who wanted to accompany them to preach were welcome. On one occasion, Ralph and a few others traveled to the very small town of Rio Frio, a banana plantation, to preach. To get there required several hours of travel on a dusty dirt road. They were in Ralph's small car without air conditioning. The only air was what came through the open windows. The tropical heat was unbearable. A total of seven people were traveling in the small Toyota.

On his return, after having preached in the meeting, it

began to rain. Suddenly in the middle of the dark road, a man appeared beckoning for Ralph to stop the car. There was a lady with him, and one could tell they were an older couple. They were not near any village, and to get to the town they were walking to would take at least another hour. When Ralph stopped, the man saw that the car was already full of people and realized that there would be no place for the two of them in the car. Ralph asked him what they needed. "My wife and I are going to the village market; we are taking our pig to try to sell it tomorrow. But if we walk the rest of the way, the pig will not weigh much and will be worth much less," the man explained.

Ralph could already imagine what the man was going to ask of him. "I wanted to know if you could take us to the village so we can be there in the morning and on time when the market opens," the man stated. So, Ralph replied: "I'm going to open the back end of my little station wagon so that you and your pig can ride along with us." Grateful, they picked up the poor pig and placed him in the back end of the car, and the old couple got in there with their animal headed for market. The car was now very full and included a pig.

Because of the rain that was now coming down heavily, they had to roll up the windows of the car. The pig got sick and had a big case of diarrhea! What a horrible experience! With this going on in the back of the vehicle, Ralph had to lower the window and stick his head out to be able to breathe. The rain was coming in and soaking him, but he continued driving until he reached the town, around 1:00AM in the morning. Even at that hour, he was able to find a small store open where he bought disinfectant. The old gentlemen took his pig out of the car and began to wash the car to remove all the excrement. He succeeded, left it well cleaned and disinfected, but none of the passengers would ever forget the experience. A sick pig in the car after going to preach.

"If it's going to be funny later, it might as well be funny now."
- *Bishop Joseph Garlington*

The uncrossable river and a tractor

In Costa Rica, the Holland family was often able to travel together throughout the country to their mission destinations. They could just get in the car and all go on mission. They began ministry in Costa Rica when Stephen was four and Kami was two years old, and two years later Tim was born. They often went to the most remote places in the country.

At that time, the roads were not paved as they are now. There are now places in Costa Rica where tourists arrive and find luxury hotels, but it was not like that when the Hollands lived and traveled together as a family. The roads were dirt and gravel, so it was often an uncomfortable and challenging trip. Sometimes there were no bridges, so they had to ford the rivers in their vehicle. There were also "hammock" type bridges, made with boards and ropes and swinging from the movement of the car as they went across. Usually, when they arrived, they slept in the little wooden churches that were built of planks cut with a chain saw from the trees growing in the area. They had no electric light and used kerosene lamps. There were also no toilets, just outhouses. To bathe, they had to go to the nearest river. But a special treat while in these remote areas was the delicious meals cooked over an open fire. There is no food as tasty as food cooked on the open fire! It has a unique and delicious flavor.

To reach one of these churches, they had to cross seven rivers. The plan was to arrive during a time when there would be no rain so that the rivers would not rise while there.

One night they had settled down to sleep in the church, and it started to rain very hard. During the night, some of the men from the church woke them up and told them that it was necessary for them to leave the area because the rivers were beginning to rise and would soon become impassable. At that time, they had a small diesel Volkswagen. They approached the river with the intention of crossing it, but once in the river, they realized the car was stranded in the river current.

Ralph got out of the car and, as he pulled the children out through the windows, he said to Donna, "Slide over behind the wheel to drive." Ralph, along with other man accompanying them, tried to push the car. Donna was sitting in the car, trying to drive a car that was a stick shift, working the clutch, trying to get out of the water that was already at waist level as she sat in the car. She was "sitting" in the water, at the wheel of the small car. The children stood outside on the riverbank praying for Mommy. Despite the great effort they made to push, Ralph realized that they would not be able to move the vehicle. They had to find a tractor to pull the car out! Donna quickly got out of the car, now almost in the middle of the river, and managed to reach the shore. Eventually, they found a man with a tractor and a rope. He pulled the car to the other side of the river, and they continued back to San Jose.

The area was very mountainous, so they had to deal with yet another problem and danger. Landslides! In that area during rainy seasons, landslides often resulted, and rocks fell from the mountains and blocked the roads. During the return trip, Ralph encountered a pile of rocks that had already slid down the mountain. The friend traveling with them got out and pushed the car while Ralph gave it all he could to get beyond the rocks. They could hear the rumbling of more rocks falling down the mountain. These young missionaries were truly adventurous. Thank God, after confronting and winning over the challenges, they made it safely back home to San Jose.

Ralph's Bridge

When Tim was just a month old, they visited some new believers who lived in the north of the country, near the Arenal volcano. This was an indigenous group of people in Costa Rica and in a very remote area. They took Tim along with them on that trip in their small Toyota. As they made their way over a dirt road, they came to a place where there was no bridge and it was not possible to just ford the small creek; it was too narrow to go down through the creek and be able to get up the other side, but that narrow creek somehow had to be crossed.

With no bridge, and the need to get across the small creek, Ralph had to think about how they could get to the other side. He quickly had an idea. He looked for two trunks of fallen trees and placed them the same distance apart as the tires of the car with the idea to use those tree trunks as a bridge. They tried and it worked. They crossed the river on that makeshift bridge made with two logs. It was one of the craziest things they did on their travels through Costa Rica! They finally got to the town of the new believers. But yes, they found another route for their return trip back to San Jose.

"Let's stay calm. This will be interesting for my book."
- ***Winston Churchill***

Donna drives fast!

On at least two occasions when Donna was driving, the Lord was obviously with her in a miraculous way. She had taken a young man and his wife to preach in the church in Turrialba. During the return that night, as was her custom, she drove her car with some "aggressiveness." Pastors sometimes laughed saying, "When we go with Pastor Donna, we don't lose any time, she drives very fast."

They were returning on a mountainous road with many curves and a lot of fog. A small truck passed them on a dangerous curve. The young evangelist who was with her said: "Pastor Donna, I can't believe you let that truck pass you because you always drive fast and don't let other cars get by! Why did you let them pass us?" As they came around the next curve, they were shocked as they came upon a very serious head-on collision. A huge truck was coming in the wrong lane and collided head-on with the small truck that had passed them back down the road. That day, Donna saw the Lord's hand of protection on their lives. She also learned the valuable lesson to take it easier on the curvy and foggy mountain roads.

Danger in high places

The Hollands often hosted mission groups from the United States. On this occasion, Ralph had rented a small bus for the group and Donna drove the pickup loaded with the suitcases along with some of the group of travelers. In that season of her life, Donna was somewhat discouraged. She wondered if the Lord was aware of her existence: "Lord, do you know where I am . . . do you even know my address?" These were days of uncertainty that she was going through in her young life.

On this day, they were on their way from San Isidro, in southern Costa Rica, to Puerto Limón, a port city on the east coast of the country. The road was mountainous. To reach the destination, they had to cross what is called the Cerro de la Muerte (the Death Pass), the highest mountain pass on the Pan American highway going up to 12,000 feet. In this geographical region, rain and fog are common. In total, eight people were traveling in the double cab and the suitcases were in the back of the pickup.

Everyone was half asleep, and Donna was driving along over the mountain pass. As she tried to maneuver one of the curves, the steering lost traction on the wet pavement. She tried her best in desperation, but the steering was out of control. There was not enough traction to make the curve; the pickup continued in a straight line towards the cliff. When she saw where they were going, she cried out in English with all her might: "Jesus!"

That woke up the passengers, and they realized they were flying in the air into the ravine. They also all began to scream, "Jesus!" Donna noticed a very small flat place and thought that the pickup would possibly stop there. However, she was unable to stop the pickup with the brake and continued further down the cliff. Eventually the pickup came to a stop and miraculously no one was hurt. Not one was injured! Donna realized that the pickup was leaning severely and could easily start to roll. She instructed her passengers to exit the vehicle on the opposite side so their weight would counter the incline and keep the truck from rolling over. When they got out of the pickup, they noticed that it had rested on a rock that held it and kept the pickup from rolling. That was the miracle! The rock had held them!

They started to climb up the cliff to the road where an ambulance happened to be passing by transporting a patient. When the ambulance driver noticed them coming up from the ravine, he stopped and asked if they were all okay. He encouraged them to get out of the rain taking refuge in a small café nearby, to rest and wait for the police and a wrecker to arrive. Ralph was following Donna in the minibus but was several minutes behind them and unaware of the accident. As the ambulance continued up the road, at Donna's request, the driver identified the bus and motioned for Ralph to stop to tell him that his wife had run the pickup in a "little hole" and that they were all fine and were waiting for them in the restaurant. Ralph, knowing the terrain of the highway, turned to the group and told them, "I don't think the pickup is in a "small hole."

When the police arrived at the scene of the accident, they asked who had been driving. Donna replied, "Me, sir." "Madam," they told her, "We congratulate you! This curve is famous because it is poorly engineered. We have seen at least thirty cars that have gone over this cliff, and yours is the only one that has not overturned." "It was God who was with us! He protected us!" she replied.

The wrecker arrived and was able to use 150 feet of cable to pull the pickup up the embankment to the road. Ralph adjusted the displaced muffler a bit, and Donna continued to drive for six more hours to Limón, on the Atlantic side of Costa Rica where they were waiting for their arrival. (Their six-year-old daughter, Kami, decided she would make the rest of the trip in the bus with her Daddy!) That day, Donna promised the Lord that she would never again doubt that He knows where she is! Never again to doubt His care and attention.

Rat races

Donna often took a young woman from the church along with her on her travels. On one of those trips, they had to sleep in the church in Siquirres. A hotel was not an option. They settled in as best they could and slept on the wooden pews of the church.

There are two things that horrify Donna: snakes and rats. That night, while sleeping in that church, the rats were racing on the exposed beams in the auditorium. They spent the night watching that show; rat races taking place above them!

Bats on the attack

Continuing with the stories of some animals that had to be dealt with along the way, on another occasion they went as a family to visit the church in Jaco Beach. This coastal city is now a tourist attraction, but at that time they had to travel several miles on a gravel road to get there. Although there were hotels, their budget did not allow them to stay in a hotel. So, the five of them had to sleep on the concrete floor of the church. They took their sleeping bags and pillows.

The pastor on location got them settled in for the night and said to them: "Pastors, I recommend that you leave the light on tonight because if you turn it off, the bats will come and have a party!" He went on to explain, "The bats love darkness and will come if there is no light; the scary thing is that before actually biting, they inject a substance like an anesthesia, and one does not realize that the bat is biting them until they wake up and see blood everywhere." That night, of course, they slept with the lights on.

Do not let go of the horse's tail

Another trip took Ralph to a rural area to visit one of the churches in the mountain. When the road came to an end, he had to leave the truck behind and continue horseback. He was met at the river and waited for his host pastor to get the horses ready. One of the men who met him approached Ralph and asked for his small suitcase which he tied to the saddle.

When Ralph was about to mount his new means of transportation, the man explained that the horse could not take another passenger across the river because of the strong current. To this comment, a very surprised Ralph, asked: "So, what do I do?" "Take off your shoes and socks and place your toes on the tendons of the horse's ankles, grab the animal's tail tightly, and hold on while crossing the strong current of the river." And so, he did just that. He crossed the river with only one determination: not to let go of that horse's tail for anything!

A family on horseback

On yet another occasion, the whole family went over the mountains to the southern zone of Costa Rica to visit another church group. This was a new group on a ranch called Morete. It was a very difficult place to get to. This time, the whole family had to leave the pickup behind and travel for almost four hours on horseback to get to the church.

They were not riding on beautiful, trained horses with a comfortable gait, but were rather on work horses. Riding on them was uncomfortable and slow. Donna and Stephen each had a horse to ride. Kami rode with one of the pastors, and Tim, who was two years old, rode in front of Ralph on the same horse with him. These were very stubborn horses and needed constant prodding.

At one point, Ralph, who was riding along behind Donna, saw a Fer-de-lance snake approaching. It is one of the most poisonous and dangerous snakes in the world and was about to pass under the horse on which Donna was riding. Ralph prayed, "Lord, don't let neither my wife nor the horse see that pit viper." Ralph knew that if the horse saw the snake, it would rear up and buck Donna off. Thank God, Donna never saw the viper nor did the horse! Donna and the horse just continued along on their journey.

They arrived, held the meeting, and returned that same night after dark, another nearly four hours on the path along the ridge of the mountain. The prayer was that the horses would not fall off the path into the ravine. They safely arrived back at the country house where they had to sleep that night. It was a wooden house without electric lights or a bathroom. When they arrived, one of the family members of that household informed them that one of the children had just been rushed to the hospital because of a scorpion bite. Once again, the Lord took care of them, and they were able to fulfill their mission.

"No hour is wasted if spent in a saddle."
- **Winston Churchill**

Speakers, hospital, and a cast

Ralph and Donna have certainly devoted all their energy to serve the Lord. They truly are Relentless! They were finishing the construction and preparing for the dedication and inauguration of the large central church building in San Jose. The pastor of the church in California that had financed most of the construction was coming to inaugurate the facility.

Ralph was rushing to finish some of the details so it would be ready for the dedication. He had worked all night painting and even placing plants in the garden to dress up the front of the new building. They wanted every detail completed with excellence. After finishing his work, he returned home to clean up and then return to the church to begin the dedication activities.

The visitors from the USA had arrived. The activity went on for three days. There was a beautiful move of God, and several new believers were baptized in the new baptistry in the church. At the end of the meeting, Ralph climbed a ladder to take down the sound system speakers. He wanted to lock them up to protect them from thievery.

Going down the ladder, he lost his balance and fell, but without letting go of the speakers. He fell to the wet tiled floor near the baptistry, and one leg went out to his side and hit the floor very hard. The speaker was saved, but his knee was badly injured. But that wasn't all. Because of lack of rest and intense work for several days, Ralph's defenses were low, and he developed strep throat. He was running a high temperature. However, he did not opt to take care of himself because he had visitors and felt that he should not abandon his responsibility to host them properly. **Relentless!**

The time came to take the visitors to the airport. One of them, seeing how sick Ralph was, told him: "Don't go home; go to the hospital to see what's going on with you." He heeded the counsel and went to the hospital. When he arrived, he was immediately hospitalized so they could administer antibiotics intravenously. He spent almost three days in the hospital.

When he thought he was about to be discharged, the doctor decided to further examine his injured knee. After doing some maneuvers, he said something that Ralph did not expect: "You are not going home! We have to operate on that knee, more precisely the meniscus." He also explained that after surgery, he would have a cast for six weeks. Laser surgery on the meniscus did not exist at that time. Ralph immediately replied: "No, it can't be. I don't have time for this now." However, on a wall of that Baptist hospital, hung a very nice painting that said, "I will give you rest." He understood that as a message from heaven; the Lord was sending him to rest.

With that full leg cast, Ralph could no longer drive around the country as he normally did. He found a solution to that immobility and said, "Maybe I can't travel to the other churches with this cast on my leg, but I don't have a cast on my tongue; I can still preach." With that decision, he began an evangelistic crusade in the central church. That year, they baptized ninety-nine people. Donna kept a count. What an awesome outcome from the decision to continue serving. Ralph could have easily used the accident as an excuse to just stay home and do nothing. Many would choose to do so. But that was not the case with Pastor Ralph. Crutches and all, he continued to preach and took the church to another level. The church experienced incredible growth. When was it? When the Lord made him rest from his usual activities and used him despite a handicap!

Complaining about a move of God

In the suburb of San Jose, Desamparados, in the location of the central church they pastored, the move of God continued. Every Sunday, there was an influx of new people and continued growth. There was great momentum and joy.

But, on one particular Sunday, a member came knocking on the office door before the service. Ralph was studying and preparing to minister. She opened the door and, about to cry, said, "Pastor, I don't like all these new people coming to our church." Ralph was very surprised and replied, "We are having a revival and new people are coming to the Lord and to the church! Why don't you like it?" She replied: "Yes, I know that, but I always sit on the aisle of the second row, in the middle section, and when I arrive for the service, someone of this new group already has my place!" Ralph closed the conversation by saying, "I'm sorry, but I don't see your name written on any bench and we haven't designated where anyone sits." And he went on to clarify to her: "You have two options; either you arrive early to take your favorite place or sit elsewhere, because I'm not going to stop what God is doing to accommodate you and your preferences." Although what happened made Ralph laugh a little, it also made him upset. Who would dare to think that the most important thing is their seating preference over a move of God?

Fighting to get in

An outstanding speaker offered to come to Costa Rica and hold a crusade. It had been announced that the he would preach about 666, the mark of the beast, the coming of the Lord, and the antichrist. Of course, everyone was interested in that subject, so about eight hundred people entered the auditorium of the main facility they had built. In the annex hall, which was the chapel in the first building they built, and which was attached to the new auditorium, they set up a monitor with remote transmission. That chapel was also filled with about two hundred more people. In total, the attendance at the crusade each night was a thousand people.

It was a tremendous success. Because of the desperation of the people to get into the event, many of them fought, not only for a place in line, but also to sit as far to the front of the auditorium as possible. Ralph could not believe what they told him: "Pastor, out in the street they are fighting because they want get in and there is no more space." Although many could not get in, that time in Costa Rica was one of great revival, countless baptisms, and many beautiful experiences of conversion.

Churches, institutes, and benches

During their time of service in Costa Rica, Ralph and Donna were able to establish seventeen churches, build buildings for many of these congregations, and set pastors in place over those churches. Many of the pastors had been trained at the Bible school founded by Ralph and Donna and located in the central church. They also discipled and mentored many young people, who were then sent out to volunteer in the new churches. They walked with these young people throughout the process. They encouraged and visited them frequently. This is how so many churches were opened during their tenure in Costa Rica. God gave them dedicated young people, very committed and passionate about the Lord and his work. That was the routine; travel, work, preach, teach, train, and motivate.

In the evenings, they taught at the Bible school, and on the weekends, they visited the new pastors in their churches. There are countless experiences! While serving as pastor of the central church, the work in the constructions of other churches was an added burden, but they moved forward - Relentless. Many times, they worked with their hands in the construction of the churches, laying blocks and raising walls for church facilities. Though laborious, it brought them much satisfaction and joy. Ralph often brought along his skill saw to make the benches. He made the pews for almost every church location! They were there to do a little of everything – out of a heart of love and service.

Everyone in the pickup

For a time, they had a double-cab Ford pickup truck with a camper top to travel around Costa Rica. It had a cover over the pickup bed, but it was not a van or a bus, it was just a pickup. To make the most of it, Ralph built small benches to go under that camper top. That allowed them to accommodate more people who wanted to accompany them on trips. These travelers were not just people wanting to go along for the ride; more specifically they were young people who also wanted to be trained in ministry. They were from both the Bible school and the church. More than once, they overloaded that pickup with too many passengers.

One of those times, was when Ralph had to visit a new church consisting of a group of indigenous people near the Turriabla volcano. On that trip, Ralph took forty people in the pickup. Yes, inside the cabin, in the camper, hanging on the running boards, sitting on the hood, and riding on the back bumper went forty people who wanted to accompany him in the ministry.

At another time, to attend an event in Guatemala, they filled the pickup with seventeen people who traveled by land from Costa Rica to Guatemala, passing through Nicaragua, Honduras and El Salvador. After the conference in Guatemala, they made the return trip to Costa Rica! What wonderful days those were! Although cramped in the pickup and uncomfortable, they traveled for hours. These were moments that trained, and marked for life, all these young people for the service of God.

"It's not enough for us to do our best. Sometimes we have to do what is required."
– *Churchill*

CALIFORNIA

Transient global amnesia

To carry out so many activities and responsibilities of missionary work, good health is not a minor detail, but quite the opposite. Unfortunately, a season of illness and weakness came into Ralph's life. Consequently, he lived through trials in his spiritual, physical and emotional life with the onset of this crisis time.

During the time they were serving in Costa Rica, Ralph began to be overwhelmed with the demands of the ministry. Gradually, the unrelenting responsibilities began to affect his health. He unwisely added too much activity, and it all took a toll on the whole man. In addition to that, when he asked for help from his mission board, they told him that he was achieving so much, and that additional help could become burdensome. He became depressed and suffered in silence. No one noticed his state of frustration. As a result, he began to make wrong and hasty decisions. They were decisions based on a depleted condition spiritually and emotionally during a time of very low self-esteem. In the process, the decisions he made hurt his family, the church, the work, and his person.

All of this finally motivated him to go to the doctor. The diagnosis was "transient global amnesia." They didn't explain the details of what that meant, but he realized that he often forgot things and sometimes "got lost." Technically it refers to a "sudden and temporary loss of memory of events that occurred during, after and sometimes before the event that caused the amnesia." There were times when he couldn't find his way home, ended up at the wrong appointments and suffered from extreme dizziness and disorientation. Ralph readily admits that the reasons for having this condition were due to a neglect of his health and, more importantly, a neglect of his time with the Lord. In addition to all of his daily ministry routines, he was also overseeing a business that had been set up to provide funds to continue to build church facilities. All these activities resulted in the collapse of his health – physically and spiritually.

He began to deviate from his purpose as a missionary. His nerves were shot, which led him to make decisions that still bring him great shame. Thank God, Donna – a strong woman – understood and sustained her husband during this complex time. She took care of him and his children, even when Ralph's reactions were completely out of character for him.

Finally, it became necessary for Ralph to remove himself from the mission field for a time. Together they returned to the United States so that he could be restored physically, emotionally, and spiritually under the care of elder ministers. Although they continued to congregate in a church, they remained out of the ministry for a short time to re-establish themselves and thus restore their life and purpose.

During the restoration process, they were in St. Louis, Missouri for a year. Donna's parents lived there, so they were a nearby resource for help in this process. At the same time, they could attend a very good church, led by a special and helpful pastor who served as an apostle and did much to restore Ralph back to an even more effective ministry. In fact, one day he rebuked Ralph saying, "You can't keep sitting here on this bench; you have to find the next place where the Lord wants to use you."

In those days, another pastor, also an apostle in their lives, offered them an opportunity to work with the Hispanic people in the state of Idaho. They agreed to take a few days and travel there to check out that opportunity. They had the trip planned, but surprisingly he called them again, now to tell them that there had been a change in the dynamics of the church, so it was not the time to start a Hispanic ministry.

An angel appears

With that detour in their plans, Ralph felt they should go to California. There they had friends in Oakland and San Jose, "We have to go there; I feel that there is a church that needs a pastor. God has something there for us," Ralph stated with confidence.

Donna agreed with Ralph, not with as much faith in what he was feeling, but as always, there by his side. They stayed at the friends' house, and Ralph went out to look for some secular work while the Lord opened the ministerial direction for them. During one of those interviews for secular employment, Donna stayed in the car reading a book. Since the car had a California license plate, coupled with the fact that she is an American, it was unlikely that anyone would think that she was not from the area.

Despite that detail, a man approached Donna's car and tapped on the window. He looked like a respectful and kind person. She, cautiously and hesitating a little, rolled down the window. The gentleman said to Donna, "Uh, you're not from here, you're here on a little vacation." Donna said to herself, "How does he know I'm not from here if the car has a California license plate?" Then he went on to say, "Well, it's not that you're here on vacation, but that you are thinking about moving here." Again, Donna wondered how that man could know that. However, the kind gentleman went on to say, "Here in San Jose, life is a bit expensive, but if you go to Gilroy or Hollister, a little further south, it's still close to San Jose and the cost of living is not as high." Donna couldn't understand why this stranger was giving her all these details. He dismissed himself saying, "Have a nice day." He turned around, got into an old car, and drove off.

"What was that about? How does he know that I am not from here? How does he know we're thinking about moving here? Are Gilroy or Hollister in California? What is the meaning of this?" These were disturbing questions that were now spinning in Donna's thoughts and, for the moment, without answers. When Ralph returned to the car from his job interview, Donna did not tell him anything about this unusual visit. She was quietly wondering how to explain what had just happened to her. That had her a little uneasy as they went to lunch together.

At lunch, they were talking to a friend, a contractor who had often helped them build churches in Costa Rica. Donna said, "Richard, are you driving clear to San Jose to attend church? It's a little far away, isn't it?" He replied, "Yes, but the other church near me is in Gilroy. That church has not had a pastor for the past two years." Then Donna said, "Gilroy? Someone just mentioned that place to me." Ralph was shocked to hear that. Donna then told him about what the man who had approached the car had told her while he was in the employment agency. "Donna, that was an angel," Ralph assured her. "No, angels don't talk to me; it couldn't have been an angel!" she replied.

They were scheduled to minister at a church near Gilroy that night. Ralph spoke to the host pastor and asked if he knew anything about a church in Gilroy that needed a pastor. "Of course!" the pastor replied. "That would be a perfect place for you: more than half of the people in the community are Hispanic, so your years in Latin America are going to help you relate with that city." The pastor put them in contact with the elder in charge of the decisions in the church in Gilroy. He asked to meet them for breakfast the next day. They met with him, they told him their story, they talked about their time in missions, and they agreed to return in two weeks to minister in the church. The church voted 100% that Ralph and Donna would be their next pastors. Within a month, they had packed up their belongings in St. Louis and moved to California.

So, in 1984, the time came to begin a new missionary destiny. California! There they had the opportunity to pastor for four years. They worked hard to build a strong church. The Lord blessed the church with growth. Along with the task of pastoring an English-language church, they started a Spanish-language church in the city of Gilroy, California. It was a good place for the transition from the denominational affiliation to a non-denominational approach to ministry. A lot of changes had to be worked through and a new vision established. It was also an opportunity for God to strengthen Ralph in this new phase of ministry. Without a doubt, God was in it all.

Through the wisdom and counsel of elder pastors, Ralph began anew and with a much more effective ministry than before his life crisis. During this time, Ralph learned so much that he felt it was important to share his experiences, and what he had learned, with others. He wrote a book entitled "Eight Sure Ways to Fail and How to Avoid Them." The book, in its second edition, was called "Failure is Not an Option."

"You can't turn back the clock, but you can wind it up again."
- Bonnie Prudden

An angel in McDonalds

On several occasions, the Lord began to confirm that He was not finished with them and that the ministry was going to continue with Hispanics, even though Ralph and Donna are obviously English-speaking Americans who at the time were living in California. One day, Ralph and Stephen were having breakfast in a "McDonalds," waiting to go set up the auditorium in the facility they rented to have service every Sunday. While they were enjoying their breakfast, they were approached by a gentleman who stopped in front of their table and, looking at Ralph, said, "You have ministered a lot with Hispanics." Ralph replied that yes, that was correct. He asked the gentleman who he was and how he knew about his past. But the stranger only replied: "Your ministry in the Spanish-speaking world is not over, but it will take on another form; it will not be like before. However, the Lord has a plan for your life, and He has it among the Hispanic people." "But who are you? Where do you live?" asked Ralph, very intrigued. "Well, I'm staying here nearby, but don't look for me because you're not going to find me." For Ralph, this was another visit from another angel sent by God to lead them on their mission.

Soon after, Ralph met a Salvadoran, in California, who invited him to come to his country to preach a crusade. This new missionary venture included a three-day crusade in the streets of a small town called Acajutla. It is port city and is always very hot. They closed the streets, built a platform in the middle of the intersection, and began to preach. What glorious days! So much so that this small event reactivated in Ralph his missionary passion, and the Lord made it clear to him that his next step would be a return to the mission field.

Donna had dropped Ralph off at the airport in San Francisco to make that trip to El Salvador. While she was driving back home, she heard an almost audible voice telling her, "Another change is coming." Of course, life was comfortable in California. They lived in a beautiful place, in a modern city with all the comfort of stateside living. Ralph had also become the director of a Christian School. In addition, he pastored a fast-growing church in which more than half of the members were Hispanic. The children were settled in their schools. But the Lord said to Donna, "A change is coming."

When Ralph returned from El Salvador, he was so blessed and encouraged to have been participating in Latin America that he proposed to Donna that, when the children finish their studies, together they would return to foreign missions. However, Donna surprised him when she said, "No, we are not going to wait for them to finish their studies." And then she told him how the Lord had already told her that another change was coming. She was ready.

At that time, Stephen was seventeen years old, Kami fifteen, and Tim eleven. Ralph and Donna sought advice from influential Mexican pastors who encouraged them to come and base in Guadalajara. This opened many doors to begin ministering in Mexico. Thank God, the children went with them without any complaints.

Stephen was so excited when he overheard his parents talking about returning to Latin America, he ran to tell his sister, Kami. At first, Kami said, "Don't tell me. No way!" However, she immediately surprised them by saying, "Okay, if you get me a puppy when we get there, I'll be fine!" Of course, upon arrival in Guadalajara, Ralph went to a vet store and returned to the house with a beautiful puppy who became part of the family. The puppy even accompanied them to Dallas and lived with them until Kami got married. Thank God for three wonderful kids; brave, willing and without complaint to serve with them in missions!

The time in California was somewhat like a testing time in the desert, of leaving the denomination, of making many changes in terms of ministerial relations, in terms of searching the Word of God about things they had taught, and to understand more clearly their new approach to ministry. There they understood much more about grace and following the voice of the Holy Spirit. Now they were dependent on God alone. There was no denominational backing or support, only full confidence that God would always be faithful. Mexico, here they come!

MEXICO

A new missionary venture, and all that it entailed, was ahead of them. They would return to missionary work, but this time in another country. The decision was to move to Guadalajara, Mexico. There they began to help pastors in the region. Rather than starting churches, their new role was to come along side and support pastors and provide leadership training. God began to develop their apostolic calling. Soon, pastors in the region were looking to them for covering and leadership.

Day-to-day provision

In Guadalajara, they served for a year and a half. This was a time of great testing and a time of minimal financial support. They knew that this was to be expected. For the twelve previous years in missions, they had the support of a denomination. Now it would be a walk by faith. The support from their stateside donors was only out of love and relationship as there was no formal commitment to do so.

As a result, difficult times came when they didn't know if they would eat the next day or if they could pay their bills; they often did not have the funds for that. On one occasion, they needed one thousand dollars to meet a pending payment. That was significant amount, so they gathered their children in their living room and everyone began to pray asking the Lord to somehow meet that need. After just a few hours, they received a call from the office that handled their finances in the United States telling them the incredible news that a pastor had called to see how he could send them an offering. He was someone who at the time, when he was invited to support them financially in the new country, scolded them for "not trusting" God's provision. The truth is that they thought they would never hear from this person again. However, now he was trying to send them an offering of a thousand dollars! Just what they needed! On another occasion, they received fifteen hundred dollars from another pastor who simply thought of them and felt to send an offering. God rewarded their obedience in surprising ways, and they experienced His miraculous provision.

Little money and a broken-down car

At a time of extreme financial need, they decided to travel as a family by car to the United States to visit the churches with the goal of raising new commitments to meet their budget and not have to live so tight. The problem was that the car they were using in Mexico was in bad condition. In fact, it was involved in an accident three days after arriving in Guadalajara, and after fixing it, it never ran well again. They knew it wouldn't last much longer.

A missionary passed by the house as they were preparing to leave and told them, "I don't know why I'm doing this because I need money too, but the Lord told me to give you this hundred-dollar bill for your trip." Ralph and Donna were beyond grateful. Encouraged by this, early in the morning they headed out on the trip through Zacatecas and along the route that passed through Saltillo, to pass near Monterrey and from there to cross the border into the United States. At that time, in Mexico it was not possible for them to use credit cards, but they could do so when they arrived at the border in Laredo. However, near Saltillo, the engine of the car burned up, and they only had a hundred dollars to repair it! The mechanics were very honest: "This car is not even worth the fix. It will cost more to fix it than it is worth."

There are realities, like the one they had just heard, that hit hard. There they were, sitting in a small hotel in Saltillo, trying to decide what to do. But, sixteen-year-old Kami, sitting at the table, said, "I feel perfect peace." The Lord spoke to them through her! Her reaction could have been one of complaint, something like "why does God have us here in these difficult times without knowing what to do?" But no, her answer expressed peace, and that's what everyone felt at the time.

Ralph then had to call immigration in Monterrey to see about being able to leave Mexico by bus and no longer in the broken-down car that had been registered in his passport. The news could not have been better; they could do it and the hundred dollars that the missionary had given them was exactly enough to buy the bus tickets from Saltillo to the border. They rode to Saltillo, walked across the border, and entered through Laredo. From there, they used their credit cards and took the Greyhound bus to their destination.

One hundred dollars is not much, but given in obedience by a fellow-missionary, for them it turned out to be a huge and miraculous amount!

I have a Van

Upon arriving in the United States, they started on tour. The questions being asked were obvious: "What are we going to do now if we don't have a car?" And even more: "How are we going to return to Mexico?" One night they were in a large church in Nashville, Tennessee, sharing about what had happened to them, how they were trusting the Lord to provide, and talking about what they had experienced throughout their time in missions.

At the end of that meeting, a gentleman approached them. He was not a member of the church, he was only visiting there that night, and told them: "I have a sixteen-passenger van, free of debt. If it will meet your needs, come by my house, and I will donate it to you." Of course, they went to his house! In that van they returned to Mexico and used it the rest of their stay in Mexico and even later when they moved to Dallas. Yes, it was one more sign that God is a God of provision!

The Van represented yet another miracle
When they moved to Dallas, they kept the van. It continued to be part of a miracle. For the first two years they lived in Dallas, they continued to depend on offerings and lived by faith.

One day, they needed to pay their credit card and decided that the best option was to sell the van since they had managed to get another car that they used in the USA. The reasoning was logical; they would sell the van because they didn't want the upkeep on two cars. That same afternoon, a gentleman was to meet Ralph with sixteen hundred dollars, which was the price they had asked for the vehicle. As the deal seemed sure, before they had the money in hand, Donna had sent the envelope with the check for the payment of the card with total peace of mind. But that afternoon, the buyer called Ralph informing him that he would not be able to buy the van. "Oh, Lord!" said Donna, "I have already sent the payment and there will be no money in the account to cover the check!" The expected remedy seemed worse than the disease.

Ralph went out that afternoon to a lake that was nearby. There he spent time in prayer and seeking God and His provision in this, another moment of crisis. When he returned, they all sat down at the table for dinner. It was five o'clock in the afternoon, and the phone rang. Ralph had left the van parked in front of a church with a very large sign that said, "FOR SALE." It was a gentleman on the phone, perhaps an angel, who said, "I see that your van has seats; I was on my way to buy another one that has no seats. I want to buy yours if you will accept the fifteen hundred dollars that I have in cash here with me." Ralph said, "Offer accepted!" They made the deposit, and the account was duly paid. That was yet another miracle of provision!

Do not despise the little because you think it is little; in the hands of God, it can be a miracle!

NICARAGUA

Ralph and Donna had frequently visited Nicaragua when they were missionaries in Costa Rica and made trips through Central America. Upon arriving in Guadalajara as missionaries, the pastor who invited them to be part of his ministry there, invited Ralph to take an overland trip with him from Guadalajara to Managua, Nicaragua. He had a Volkswagen van with no seats. He had gathered many supplies to take to Nicaragua. In 1988, Nicaragua suffered from great poverty and scarcity. He explained to Ralph: "We have to go by land because there is a lot we need to take, including a significant offering for the pastors in Nicaragua." However, he explained, it will be necessary to make the trip in December, during the Christmas season.

At first, Donna struggled a lot with that timing. The family had just moved from California to Guadalajara. She said to the Lord, "I have always been willing to share my husband with whatever need, and without complaining, but why this at Christmas time?" And the Lord, in an almost audible voice, said to her, "Let him go!" Donna surrendered to the plan and told Ralph to go with her blessing, and that she would look for a way to spend Christmas with her children. Ralph suggested that Donna take them across the border to spend Christmas with her family in the United States, while he would accompany the pastor to Nicaragua. "Then we will get together to celebrate our family Christmas time, even if it's on another date," he concluded.

Ralph and the pastor from Guadalajara traveled by land throughout Mexico, crossed Guatemala, El Salvador and Honduras and finally arrived in Nicaragua in the VW van, which, by the way, was minus any luxury features. They arrived in the village of Diriamba, where a beautiful family received them. Ralph fell in love with that family. There was an immediate connect and bond with the couple and their eleven children.

Upon returning to Mexico, Ralph traveled to the United States to meet Donna and the kids. Ralph already knew that there was now a strong link to Nicaragua in his spirit, and that one day, his plan would be to continue traveling to Nicaragua to support that ministry.

A few months later, in Dallas, the pastor of the church where Ralph and Donna eventually served as mission pastors told Ralph, "I want to accompany you to Nicaragua, but I don't want to go to Managua. I want to preach a crusade on the outskirts, in a town where few would go to preach." Ralph answered him with all certainty: "Well, I have the place. Let's go to Diriamba." They followed through with that plan and arrived with a small team from the church in Dallas. The crusade was attended by around a thousand people. During the day, they took advantage of the opportunity to do a leadership seminar for pastors.

On that trip, the heart of the pastor of the megachurch in Dallas was connected to Nicaragua. He told Ralph, "I want our church to accept Nicaragua as our adopted nation," and from then on, the Lord provided leadership and a team in Nicaragua. The Mundo de Fe ministry (the Spanish name for the network led by the Hollands) came to be known throughout the country. They often gathered hundreds of pastors and leaders in a very all-inclusive opportunity for the churches throughout Nicaragua.

Many denominations, independent pastors, and church leaders began to count on these regular activities and events. After ten years of doing leadership conferences, the decision was made to build an example church for that entire nation. A beautiful facility, one of the largest in the country, was built in Managua.

Sometimes Donna humbly wonders what would have happened if she had asked Ralph not to go, but rather to stay with her and the kids to celebrate Christmas. If she had done that, perhaps none of what exists in Mundo de Fe Ministries today in Nicaragua would have happened. How important it is to value every opportunity and every open door the Lord gives us! Often what seems to be so humble, like the family in Diriamba, can lead to an opportunity to make an impact on an entire nation!

Don't steal my blessing

"Mama Nubia" is the founder of the "Donna Holland" school in Diriamba. It was with her and her family that connections began in Nicaragua. At the beginning of this time, when Ralph was just getting to know this precious family, he came as a simple missionary to visit and encourage them in a time of extreme poverty in Nicaragua.

Later, when going to Nicaragua from Dallas, even though they themselves lived with limited resources, Ralph wanted to visit Nicaragua and support this family. On one occasion, while on his return to the airport, Mama Nubia approached Ralph and respectfully holding his hand, placed something in it. Opening his hand, Ralph saw that she had given him a twenty-dollar bill. Ralph immediately said to her: "No, I can't accept it. In fact, I came to help you, and not to receive anything; I cannot accept this offering." "Pastor Ralph, you are not going to rob me of the blessing that will be mine for sowing this seed," she replied. Now Ralph had no other choice than to receive that offering of love. It was a small offering, but from Nubia it was very significant. With some reluctance, but understanding the spiritual principle, Ralph received the twenty dollars.

From then on, Mama Nubia and her family have been greatly blessed. Many have supported the vision of the school, the ministry of her and her husband by building a small building for their barrio church, and a church in the USA blessed them with a new house. It was only twenty dollars. That seed sown by a woman in such poverty, has resulted in such a great blessing to her personally, her family, and the school that she later founded.

The "Donna Holland" School

After beginning the ministry in Nicaragua, Ralph and Donna had identified a gift in Mama Nubia, a humble woman who only had a fourth-grade education. It had to do with her ability to receive a vision and make things happen that are impactful for the Kingdom of God."

Soon after building the relationship with the Hollands, she decided to start a pre-kinder in their humble church building in Diriamba. This was, of course, done with the blessing of her husband, the pastor of that congregation. That small facility had been built by Ralph and some men from New York on a short-term mission trip to Diriamba. And there, the new educational challenge was undertaken.

Beginning with pre-kinder, Nubia asked permission to call it the "Donna Holland Christian School." By the way, Donna did not feel worthy of her name identifying a school, but knowing that it was Nubia's wish, she agreed.

That school began to be an impact on that community of extreme poverty, and by faith, each year they expanded to include more grades. First, second, third and so on. After twenty years, today it includes a high school from which many students have continued to university studies. It is officially recognized by the government and, at times, has had more than five hundred students enrolled in a school year. It is a school in humble facilities, educating very humble students who come from very poor neighborhoods. Many do not have the financial ability to even attend the public schools. If it were not for the school, the need for education would not be met in their lives. Through the school, not only do they receive a quality education, but also a Christian education.

Nubia's daughters and granddaughters are also involved in the school. Two of them have learned English very well and began to serve as translators for mission groups arriving in Nicaragua. In fact, a lot of people in those groups have provided scholarships for students. So, through the years, it has been a ministry truly developed by faith.

The Lord has provided for this humble woman, Nubia, who obeyed God's vision and stood firm, always believing, even though on many occasions the lack of resources threatened to close the school. Mama Nubia is a good match with Ralph and Donna as she too is Relentless! Always, and in some miraculous way, the Lord has continued to bless the school and, through the school, the entire community of Diriamba! (If you would like to sponsor a student in the school, please contact the Hollands by email.)

What a wonderful lesson for Ralph and Donna! Oh, how the Lord can use the most humble who are obedient to what He calls them to do, without pretexts, without excuses. Nubia is someone who could well present excuses and pretexts for unbelief and doubt rather than stepping out in faith for such an endeavor. Why? Because she has eleven children of her own! They are already adults, of course, and now she also has many grandchildren and great-grandchildren. She is now an elderly woman, but she is still there, supporting, encouraging, inspiring. Her daughters provide leadership for the school, while she prays! When there is a need, they call "Mama Nubia," as they respectfully call her, to pray and ask the Lord to provide. She is a great lesson in faith and how to be a blessing and impact the life of the community where she and her husband served as pastors until his passing.

Mundo de Fe – Nicaragua!

It is very difficult to describe and explain the national impact that the Lord has allowed in Nicaragua through Mundo de Fe. The ministry is blessed with facilities that can accommodate leaders from all over the country for their annual conference and other events. They have been blessed by visits from three presidents of Nicaragua in the national events. The impact through television and radio has reached the entire country. But the main thing is the power of the Word that has resulted in transformed lives and strengthened the body of believers throughout the nation.

BETWEEN THE NORTH & SOUTH POLES!

The message he didn't preach

Ralph was invited to minister at a conference in a country "between the North Pole and the South Pole" in a church located on the outskirts of a major city. Some pastors agreed to invite Ralph after having seen his television program that was broadcast throughout Latin America.

When Ralph arrived at the airport, two pastors met him and told him that they were going directly to the event venue. They arrived and seated Ralph on the front row as the guest speaker. The auditorium was full, and the service was about to start. The meeting began with some very traditional songs common to the area. They then introduced a trio of singers with guitars who sang some very nice folk songs, but they did not have much spiritual impact. After them, came another very similar trio that sang for half an hour and even repeated songs already sung by the first group.

As the service progressed, the host pastor informed Ralph that he would need to finish his preaching at nine o'clock sharp that evening because many had taken public transportation to get there, and the last bus would leave at 9:10PM. Ralph assured him that would be no problem. At this point in the service, the second group was still participating. Then, someone went up to receive an offering, which took up more time since he not only took the offering but preached a short message. As if that were not enough, while receiving the offering he invited one of the trios to come back with one more song.

At 8:55 in the evening, they introduced Ralph to preach. He went up to the platform, not forgetting the pastor's instructions to finish on time, and stood at the pulpit. He quickly thanked the host pastors for the invitation, and to everyone's shocked said, "Now, everyone please stand and we will be dismissed." Many of those present began shouting, "Preach, Preach!" To which Ralph replied: "No, for various reasons I will not preach tonight:

1. I'm tired from traveling all day to get here.
2. I am very upset and do not want to preach out of my anger.
3. The trios that dominated the service with songs that contributed nothing to true worship, are now outside. I see them standing out there in the street, drinking their sodas, laughing, and talking.
4. I respect the pastor's word to finish at nine o'clock, and I will cooperate."

"Come tomorrow, I will be in a better mood, and we will have a good time in the Word." The silence in the auditorium was astounding. He prayed to close out the meeting, and when he came down from the platform, many pastors approached him apologizing and telling him that he had taught them a great lesson.

So, Ralph claims that the best message he ever preached at a conference is the message he didn't preach!

Almost serving as a "Doctor" in Costa Rica

In the north of Costa Rica there is a peninsula called

Nicoya. There was no road in good condition to get there, so Ralph had to cross over on a ferry. When he arrived on the peninsula, he walked a few miles on a dirt path from where he left the vehicle. There was a small group of believers waiting to be baptized. After the service, Ralph slept on the floor of the hut.

When he awoke the next morning, he noticed a small group of people talking with a man and his wife with a small child. The pastor introduced them to Ralph. He then asked him to do them the favor of taking the wife to the hospital in the nearest town because she was about to give birth and was already having labor pains. Ralph immediately agreed. They walked the five miles to the pickup for the trip to the hospital.

To Ralph's surprise, when they arrived at the truck, the husband said goodbye to his wife and explained to Ralph that he had to stay with their small children that they had left at home and could not accompany his pregnant wife to the hospital. What a situation! Ralph with a pregnant lady and a baby about to be born right there. As they drove over the gravel road, her labor pains increased. With every bump in the road new cries of pain were heard. Ralph started driving even faster; he didn't want to be the "midwife." Thank God, they managed to get to the hospital, and, in less than thirty minutes, a beautiful baby was born.

"Doctor" Holland in Ghana

Emmanuel was the host missionary for a trip to Ghana. In addition to the leadership conferences held in Ghana and Nigeria, Emanuel also ships equipment to hospitals and clinics. He provides renovations in hospitals because of the extreme deterioration of the facilities. He had done some updates to a maternity clinic in Accra, Ghana. While Ralph was in Accra, Emmanuel wanted Ralph him stop by the clinic to see the remodeling he had done.

Emmanuel had other things to do so he left Ralph in the clinic after having introduced him to the director. Emanuel had introduced him as "Doctor Holland." Ralph entered the clinic, and after a brief dialogue, the director, who was the main midwife, invited Ralph to see the remodeled project. They left her office to go to a room where, to Ralph's surprise, there were three maternity beds with three women suffering intense labor pains! They kept walking to the other room, the one that was being remodeled, where there were also women waiting their turn to go to the delivery room.

Ralph toured the entire facility. His concern was that on his way out he would have to go back through the delivery room where the three women were screaming in pain. He looked for another exit from the facility, but he found none. As they entered the delivery room, the nurse midwife noticed that one of the babies was about to be born, so she stopped and said, "Doctor Holland, can you assist me? Help me with this tub of water to put the baby in after birth." He followed her instructions. Once the baby was born, she asked: "Do you want to cut the umbilical cord?" Without hesitation, Ralph replied, "No, you better do it."

Lesson learned: If you are going to use the title of "Doctor of Theology," please make sure that it does not include the obligation to be a midwife.

Crossing Borders: From Haiti to the Dominican Republic
Haiti is the poorest country in the western hemisphere. Ralph still carries a burden and feels a calling and responsibility to continue ministry there as he did fifty years ago. The need is so great, and very little progress is being made to better that country.

A few years ago, there was a devastating earthquake that left thousands dead and destroyed many structures, including the church, school, and pastor's home that Ralph and Donna support. Thank God, there was no loss of life among the ministry team. More recently, they have suffered floods, hurricanes and another earthquake, added to another unknown number of deaths due to the COVID-19 pandemic.

Haiti shares the island with the Dominican Republic.

On one of Ralph's more recent trips to Haiti, he made the decision to go by land from Haiti to the Dominican Republic, thinking it would be cheaper than flying. Kindly, the pastor took him in his Jeep to the border, traveling over unpaved roads that in many sections were flooded by rains.

He left Ralph at the border that had to be crossed by walking through the muddy terrain. The distance between the two borders is about one mile of no-man's land. There were boys who, in exchange for a tip, could cross a passenger from one border to the other on their small motorbikes. Ralph climbed on one of the motor bikes, while the chauffeur of another bike grabbed his suitcase. They rode, jumped, and slipped in the mud. Ralph was so frightened by the environment, by the poor mode of transportation and for his own personal safety, that he sent a picture of all that spectacle to Donna just in case he was kidnapped or disappeared from the map.

Once the immigration process was completed, Ralph eagerly sought a new means of transportation to take him on the four-hour trip to Santo Domingo. An individual showed up in his own car, saying that it was a taxi and that he could take him. Ralph inquired about the cost, but the answer was, "Don't worry about it, we'll work that out on the road." They started the journey. While they proceeded away from the border crossing, Ralph kept insisting that he tell him the price for his service. Ralph felt that he was in a situation where the driver would take advantage of him. For that reason, Ralph ordered him to stop the car and let him out. The man did not want to let him out. However, on a corner where he had to slow down, Ralph did not hesitate and jumped out of the car!

He immediately ran into a person who informed him of a bus service that was going to Santo Domingo. He told Ralph that the bus had already left the terminal but had not gone very far yet. Off in the distance, Ralph saw the bus still picking up passengers, so he was able to run and catch up with it. He managed to get on board, but he did have to sit next to a drunk woman. The loud music, the woman with a few alcoholic drinks, and the disputes between several passengers made the trip unforgettable.

Later, the driver had to stop and literally "kick" a passenger off the bus. Ralph was left thinking that now the trip could be a little quieter. Instead, the bus was speeding forward and couldn't help but hit and kill a cow! The poor animal died on the spot. People started screaming for the driver to stop and pay for what he had done, but he sped up to escape from there and not have to pay the owner for the cow. And, to make matters worse, a few more miles down the road, the bus had a flat tire.

Finally arriving in Santo Domingo, Ralph thought that the worst of his trip was over. But wait, there's more! The terminal was in a very dangerous part of the city. When Ralph got off to wait for those who would come to pick him up, fights and blows broke out again at the bus station. Thank God, after about fifteen minutes the hosts arrived to pick him up and "rescued" him from an odyssey he would never want to repeat.

Crossing Borders: From Costa Rica to El Salvador

Living in Costa Rica, the Holland family, Ralph, Donna five months pregnant with Tim, Stephen, and Kami, planned a trip by land to El Salvador. The plan was to arrive in that country through Nicaragua and Honduras. They left San José a little late in the afternoon, with the goal to at least get to Managua, the capital of Nicaragua that evening.

They arrived at the border just five minutes after the border offices had closed. They had traveled four long hours from San José to the border, including the road that for the last 50 miles was dirt and gravel. They soon realized that for nothing in the world would they be allowed to exit Costa Rica and enter Nicaragua. The border had closed, and the authorities were not about to let them through. Ralph literally begged the officials and guards to allow them to cross, considering that Donna was five months pregnant and traveling with two young children aged four and six. When they threatened to throw him in the little jail at the border crossing if he kept insisting, he gave up. They were not allowed to cross.

There was no choice but to accept what would be their accommodations for that night. In their little car, they prepared to spend the night until eight in the morning, when the border would open again. In that very hot tropical climate, they spent the night without air conditioning and with the windows closed for security. When they had no choice but to lower the windows for some fresh air, they were invaded by mosquitoes of all sizes entering the car; even a cow that was walking around stuck its head in the open window. The closed windows produced an unbearable confinement and a heat as if it were literally an oven. It was one of the most miserable nights of their entire lives.

The next day they were able to cross, but they had to drive late that night to get to San Salvador on time. They spent almost a whole day traveling after crossing the border of Nicaragua until they arrived in El Salvador, extremely fatigued. But it was well worth it to spend times of encouragement with fellow missionaries. They just consider it as another one of those "missionary journeys."

LEARNING EXPERIENCES

In 1969, after graduation, Ralph and Donna left the Bible college to live in Detroit for two years on an "internship." The Bible college offered them another certificate in addition to the diploma already obtained. They were very blessed by this opportunity; it allowed them to serve alongside a pastor in Michigan who was very involved in missions. He was a pastor with a big missionary heart and highly respected as a man of strong principles. His influence on Ralph and Donna was significant. In addition to ministry training, he was instrumental in launching them into foreign missions in 1971.

Clean the baptistry, please

As part of his service alongside the pastor and mentor, there were some responsibilities that Ralph had to accept that would develop his character. One of them, which Ralph greatly enjoyed, was preaching. He wanted to preach and hoped that the pastor would give him his chance, since that was what he felt he had prepared for in Bible college.

But instead of being asked to preach, he was assigned the responsibility to clean the baptistry. Yes, drain the water that had been used in that significant act of obedience and clean the baptistry for the next baptismal service. There was the future preacher, cleaning the baptistery. As he was in there scrubbing it, he kept thinking, reflecting, and concluding, "I didn't go to Bible college to do this. Why doesn't this pastor recognize my ability to preach and give me more important assignments than this?" However, he kept scrubbing; he soon realized how important it is to learn to obey in even the humble and insignificant opportunities in the ministry. What a great lesson was learned as he finished that task! It wasn't just about being an awesome pulpit preacher, but of being a preacher serving in the trenches who also from time to time preaches behind a pulpit.

Learning at the funeral home

Under the leadership of that same pastor, was a very sobering experience, and yet one that every pastor must be prepared for, happened for Ralph. One day, a local funeral home called the church office asking for a pastor to do a funeral. The senior pastor was the ideal person, but he was unavailable. The office suggested that another pastor could go in his place. So, who did they entrust with the task? Ralph. Yes, the pastor sent him to officiate at what would be his first funeral. The family of the mourners was not from the church, but they wanted a pastor to help them by doing a service in honor of the family member who had passed away.

Although it may seem simple, it is not so simple for someone who has never spoken in a situation as special and sensitive as that of a family that mourns a loved one and must say goodbye. Ralph was a bundle of nerves. He was only twenty-two years old and had no idea how to fulfill that ministerial role. He arrived for the funeral and spoke with the relatives, to whom he asked, "Do you have any special requests for this service, such as a special song, a poem, a testimonial from a family member, etc.?" But the family said, "We have no idea, just conduct it like you always do." What they didn't know was that Ralph had never officiated in a funeral! All went well, and Ralph added another experience to his ministerial development.

Hippies, LSD and the Gospel

One of the ministries that Ralph helped develop in the church in Detroit took place in the inner-city. At that time, in 1970, there were many druggies in the city. In many of the public parks, young people congregated in the evenings. Drugs were sold openly all over the park with the vendors announcing what drugs they had for sale. About a thousand young people usually met in a certain park.

This was seen by the church as an opportunity to do missionary work among them, right there in the city. The church bought a house downtown and, after remodeling it, turned it into a rehab place for drug addicts. Ralph and other men from the church went to the park every week to mix among the young people. It was the time of the "hippies," with Beatles music loudly playing all over the park. These were very liberal young people, very relaxed, sitting in groups, discussing their philosophies. Ralph would sit in one of those groups and listen to them. He quickly entered their conversations using that opportunity to tell them about Jesus.

It was his missionary heart that pushed him to mingle among them and share the gospel. One day the police arrived and arrested hundreds of the young people, publishing in the newspaper the next day the names and addresses of everyone they had arrested. The surprise was to learn that many were from the affluent sectors of the city of Detroit. Their parents gave them money to spend on whatever they wanted. The parents basically wanted the kids out of house. Ralph arranged to take several of them to the rehab center to recover from their drug addiction. Certainly, that was also a training ground for Ralph in reaching out to those in desperate need of love, direction for their life, and rehabilitation.

Dangerous puddings

Ralph has never been a fearful person. When they lived in Puerto Rico and served as missionaries, the Bible school decided to sell what they call "puddings." The best market for sales was in the public housing apartments. The students organized into groups and went out to make sales, which helped finance the Bible school and certain activities for the students. If a pudding was sold at the price of one dollar, the profit was fifty cents.

One day Ralph decided to go to a housing project near the San Juan airport to sell puddings. He later learned that this was the most dangerous place under the US flag. (Remember, Puerto Rico is a territory of the USA.) A gentleman stopped him and said, "I don't think you understand the danger you're in. This place is dangerous and even more so seeing that you are a white American." And he went on to say, "They'll think you have money because you're selling puddings; you're in serious danger here, and you don't speak much Spanish." But Ralph laughed, although he later decided to change clientele! Though not fearful, he learned to use wisdom in such situations and not create unnecessary incidents!

Although these are stories from his youth, the truth is that not much has changed. Even at a much more mature stage of life, he continues to be much the same, without fear and cowardice. There are still times of danger, as was the case on a recent trip to Greece with his family. Two men tried to rob him on the street. Not to be outdone, when one of them put his hand in Ralph's pocket to take his money, Ralph went on the attack and saved his wallet.

MUNDO DE FE (FAITH WORLD)

At the beginning of Mundo de Fe, the Spanish-speaking ministry founded by Ralph and Donna in Dallas, Ralph led a Wednesday night Bible study. He had a guaranteed congregation of three ladies, and two of them were named Margarita! Later, one of them was very supportive alongside Donna in the Women's Ministry; another currently serves in Mundo de Fe, with her husband, as care pastors. The third woman was very faithful, but she always came to the meetings very drunk. That is why Ralph humorously says that he started Mundo de Fe with "two Margaritas and an alcoholic."

Mundo de Fe and God's Provision

When they arrived in Dallas, the idea was for Donna to work in the office of a mission agency that had invited her to an administrative position while Ralph would continue traveling to Mexico and Nicaragua. Living in Dallas would allow the children to continue their studies in the United States. But missions was still their calling, especially for Ralph.

At that time, the children were still at home and Donna

felt the responsibility to both be with the kids and serve in ministry. Shortly after their relocation to Dallas, they began attending a church that at the time was called Faith World. Later the name was changed to Covenant Church. Ralph continued with his travels and ministering someplace most every weekend.

Five months had passed since arriving in Dallas, and while Ralph was on a trip to Nicaragua, there was a Sunday night when a ministry traveling family, known for their singing, visited the church. That night, after they sang, the pastor said, "This family has dedicated their lives to serve the Lord; we are going to give them an offering of five thousand dollars." One couple stood up and said, "We want to add a thousand dollars to that." The offering that night was six thousand dollars for the ministry family.

After the service, the pastor and the ministry guests invited Donna to go eat with them, but she very cordially turned down the offer and returned home. The real reason was that she had no money. That week, she felt that she should fast, taking advantage of the fact that Ralph was not there. Her need for answers from the Lord was urgent. She was very discouraged and frustrated with their lack of finances for the ministry they felt they were called to do.

A church in Tennessee had called them to inquire about the possibility of them going there to pastor that church. Ralph did not have much peace with that possibility because he always felt more inclined to missions. But the option was not ruled out. "Lord," Donna prayed, "tell us if it is your will that we go there; I need you to clearly show me the answer. Otherwise, we will have to see your hand on our lives for the provision we need." They were not living with luxuries, they had not bought a house, they were just renting with the basics they had. They needed the Lord to show up and confirm His direction in this move to Dallas. So, Donna continued in prayer: "Lord, this singing family received that big offering; help me to bless them and not to be jealous or envious of what has happened for them. Lord, show us your will and confirm it with your provision!"

Later that week, Ralph returned from Nicaragua and

joined the family for church that Sunday. In the service, the pastor called on Ralph: "I want you to share about your trip to Nicaragua this week." As the pastor called Ralph to the platform, he said, "Have the whole family come up here with you." And so, they did.

The pastor's prayer over the family was powerful, and, without knowing he was doing so, he even mentioned details that Donna had asked about in prayer that week. After his prayer, he told the congregation: "This family has been attending here, and now consider this their home church. Ralph continues to travel in missions, and we haven't really supported them financially. We are going to commit to six months of support at one thousand dollars per month." A total of $6000! And he went on to say, "They could go anywhere in this nation to pastor a church and live a more comfortable lifestyle, but they would be out of God's will if they decided to do that."

That Sunday, they gave them the pledged support of $6000 plus an extra thousand that very day. After that meeting, the pastor invited them to go eat. At the end of the meal, he told his wife: "Write them the first check for a thousand dollars, because surely they need it." And they did need that check! They were able to repair the van to make a trip to Mexico that they still had pending because they did not know when or how they could budget to go.

Opportunities and moments like this served to strengthen not only their faith, but also that of their children who clearly saw God's hand and provision over their lives. A few months later, the pastor decided to appoint them as mission directors for the church. That was a year after arriving in Dallas. About six months later, the pastor felt that the church needed a Hispanic ministry, so he invited Ralph to start the Hispanic congregation Mundo de Fe!

That was the beginning of Mundo de Fe Ministries that, at the time of this writing, is celebrating their 30th ministry anniversary. When the pastor extended the invitation to be the founder of this ministry, Ralph replied: "Pastor I know how to work as a team. I love it, I want to serve as much as possible, but remember that what I do best is missions.

I am here to serve in whatever other area as well, but do not forget that my best function, where I have the most effectiveness, is in missions." This was in fulfillment of a pledge Ralph had made upon leaving California. He had made the decision not to accept any opportunity to pastor that would prevent him from working freely in missions.

With this new challenge in the Dallas area, and after so many years during which the Lord had taken them from one place to another, they were able to settle down and, among other things, finally own their own home.

A Doctorate and a travel agency

When they pastored in California, the church was already established and gave them a comfortable salary, which was a blessing. However, Donna opted to look for secular employment at that time. She believed it was important to do so because there had been a lot of transitions for them, and they were restarting their lives. She wanted to work and help Ralph supply the finances for the household. The kids were now older, and she felt a release to work outside the home.

But, without knowing at the time, this was also ordered by the Lord who knows the end from the beginning. She felt strongly impressed to take a course to prepare to work in the travel industry. For three years, she worked as a travel agent. She organized trips for groups of clients, she learned everything related to travel, airline tickets, hotel bookings, excursions, and cruises. Sometimes she would say, "Lord, I have been a missionary for twelve years, and here we are pastoring a church. Why do you have me working in a travel agency?"

Although she didn't understand all the reasons why, she felt that was what she needed to do at the time. A few years later, she understood why she had prepared for what lay ahead in her ministry. For many years now, their life has been traveling, organizing mission trips, taking groups on missions, planning flights, hotels, their own trips, and added to that the eight tours of Israel that they have organized for more than twelve hundred people. The Lord prepared her for all of this. She listened to that "still small voice" when, at the moment, she did not yet have the full picture.

Ralph also had taken advantage of the time in Gilroy to continue his studies at San José State University while serving as the director of a Christian School. All of this contributed to his resume. While in Dallas, and with taking just a few more classes, he was able to obtain his Doctorate at Primus University where they accepted his life map which included a year at the University of Tennessee, three years of the Bible college, his internship in Detroit, his studies in California, his mastering of the Spanish language, and having authored a book.

Ralph and Donna are amazed at all that has developed during their time in Dallas. They tremble to think of where they would be if they had not been sensitive to the direction of the Lord that led them to Dallas. Mundo de Fe would not be a reality. Many missionaries would possibly not have been mentored and sent out which happened under their leadership as missions pastors in a large English-speaking congregation, while at the same time they pastored Mundo de Fe.

From Mexico, they had wanted to move to San Antonio or even Austin, but they didn't feel peace with those options. They felt a strong confirmation of the Holy Spirit when they considered settling in Dallas. They knew they would be serving someplace, and in some way, but not with the extensiveness that the Lord has allowed them to serve. As missions pastors, the door was opened to reach into the nations of Latin America and other countries such as Spain, Turkey, Cambodia, India, Russia, Indonesia, Singapore, Thailand, Africa, and so many places where the Lord has given them the opportunity to serve alongside missionaries and provide covering and oversight for many. None of that would have been possible if the Lord had not so carefully and patiently led them to Dallas.

Beware of what you say you never want to do ...

It is so important to learn to listen to the soft voice of the Holy Spirit and not get sidetracked along the way. This is true even in difficult times, when everything seems to be against you, and there is uncertainty as to from where God's direction and provision will come. There are moments of doubt, which we all go through. Dallas was a gift from God, but their eventual arrival there was not what Ralph and Donna would have ever imagined. The interesting, and now rather humorous mention, is that many years ago Ralph had declared three things he never wanted to do in ministry:

1. To be a missionary in Mexico; it seemed to him that there were other countries more in need of American missionaries.

2. He never wanted to live in the United States and from there do missions work; he felt that was living the best of both worlds to live the comfort of the United States and travel from there to do missions. He believed that if he was to be a missionary, he must live in a foreign country.

3. Even though he speaks Spanish fluently, he declared that he never wanted to pastor a Hispanic congregation in the United States.

He has done all three of these things he "never wanted to do." Yes, you must be very careful with what you say and even more when you say it to God. They have served for many years in Mexico and have a deep love for its people and culture. They live in the United States and travel to other countries to do missions. They have not only pastored a Hispanic congregation in the United States, but they are the founders of the Mundo de Fe Network.

Never say never. You can so easily bypass the Will of God and the plans He has for your life. It is certainly better to always be attentive, alert, and subject to His will. That may mean that you must put aside your own ideas that are often encumbered with plans that are not in tune with what God desires. Just follow the direction of the Holy Spirit. Mundo de Fe Ministries is what it is today due to two main factors:

1. The opportunities that the Hollands had to visit and live in many of the countries of origin that are represented in the network of Mundo de Fe Ministries: Mexico, Puerto Rico, Dominican Republic, Costa Rica, Nicaragua, El Salvador, Guatemala, Honduras. The Lord took all that experience early in Ralph and Donna's ministry and helped them found what is today a large central church, which at one point came to have representation of every country in Latin America and Spain among the congregants.

2. The Plan of God. God declared that it would be so. Shortly after being involved in a car accident in Guadalajara, they attend a ladies' event. Ralph and another pastor sat in the back. Donna listened attentively to the Word. The guest speaker gave a very impactful message about faith. Ralph was deeply moved by her message. At the close of the meeting, while he was headed in her direction to greet the lady that had ministered and thank her for the encouragement he had received from the message, she came directly to him and said to him: "I don't know who you are, or where you come from or what you are doing here, but the Lord told me to tell you that He is going to give you a very "visible" ministry throughout Latin America. "And just how is this going to happen? But he received the Word.

The day that the Hispanic Congregation began, part of the group that promised to help start the church were family members of the founder of the Enlace TV network. At this point Enlace was just starting up in Costa Rica in a small house and with a signal that reached no more than the neighborhood that housed the studio. Through the relationship with the founders of Enlace, and the family members who attended Mundo de Fe, they offered Ralph airtime on the channel. As a result, he had a program on Enlace for twenty years. The fulfillment of that word that Ralph would have a very "visible" ministry!

The channel soon reached the world and as a result, Mundo de Fe became known throughout Latin America. Many came to the church saying that they had seen on Enlace that there was a church in Dallas and that the pastor had a very good program on the network. Others came to Mundo de Fe in Dallas because their relatives in Latin America had told them about Mundo de Fe through the program on Enlace. The Lord said it would be visible in Latin America, and as always, he was correct! He just had not told them at the moment how He would do it, but it happened.

"Continuous effort, not strength or intelligence, is the key to unlocking our potential."
- Churchill

PART 5

BEYOND LATIN AMERICA

Later, they were given a word of prophecy that they could not disregard; it was specific and guiding. They knew it came from God, but it was also hard to believe because it was a time of great scarcity of funds, with teenage children, with hardly any budget with which to operate. Their faith was challenged to believe such a strong prophetic word.

They attended a meeting in Houston. They were still residing in Mexico at the time. The word that was given over them seemed so unlikely, but it seemed so correct. "You are going to go in and out of many countries of the world, way more than you can imagine. Do not worry! The funds will be available for this new task." Exciting! They did not reject the word, but it was difficult for them to imagine the fulfillment of it at that time, although today they celebrate it with great joy and gratitude. Trust in that word has always sustained them.

The truth is that if they had not remained faithful in those moments of trials that few can imagine, they would not have seen themselves traveling extensively, going and coming, and almost living in airplanes as they go from one country to another.

THE MISSIONS NETWORK

For thirty years, Donna has been leading what is called *International Missions Network.* In part, one reason for the move to Dallas was because of an invitation from the ministry that had provided administrative assistance and covering over them since they had moved from California to Guadalajara, Mexico. The director of that agency recognized Donna's gift of administration. Through the administrative responsibilities that she had experienced while they lived abroad, she already understood a lot of the details and dynamics of what is required to assist in the administrative life of someone who lives and serves in another country. This includes tasks such as receiving and depositing funds, reporting to the government, taxes, and a whole world of details that often differ from country to country. Knowing that there were many missionaries who needed this service that Donna could handle very effectively, the director's invitation was not long in coming: "Would you like to help me in the home office for the agency in Texas?" She accepted, and once they arrived in Dallas, Donna began working in that office. She did so for two years, while together with Ralph, they continued their missions involvements and later became a part of Covenant Church.

As their involvements in the Dallas area shifted, the opportunity came to assume another 501c-3 (non-profit charter) that was ideal to serve as a new mission agency directly under her leadership. She was able to have it up and running in three days. Many of their missions associates asked to be a part of this new agency. To this day, she serves several missionaries, helping them serve in the countries to which God has called them, and relieving them of the worry of the administrative details here in the United States. For over thirty years, she has continued to provide this service to many who serve all over the world.

Ralph and Donna's missionary focus had always been the Caribbean, Central America, Mexico and a few trips to South America. When they became mission pastors in a mega church in Dallas, the whole world opened to them. Even more so as the church became known for its strong emphasis on missions under the Holland's leadership. Many with a call to mission service came there looking for direction.

Of course, they were directed to the missions office to share their vision, their passion, their calling, their needs, and to see how to implement what the Lord had told them to do. Thanks to the large budget dedicated to missions by the church, Ralph and Donna were not only able to guide them, but also visit them on location in the country where the Lord had called them to serve. This gave them an opportunity to become familiar with and identify with the cultures of Europe, Africa, and Asia, areas very different from those they had served in Latin America. The love for missions, that had been exclusive to Latin America now extended beyond what they had previously known.

AFRICA

Conference, books and twenty dollars

The Congolese foreign minister once said, "You have to visit the Congo to really understand it." He was right! It is a region where there is a lot to learn. Ralph and Donna's first trips to Africa were to the Congo, perhaps the poorest and most oppressed of African nations. The time they served in Haiti certainly prepared them to be able to adapt to the experience of ministering in Africa.

They were given the opportunity to minister at an incredible conference with seven thousand pastors present from all over the Congo. This was a unique experience that exposed them for the first time to the worship culture in Africa. However, even though the believers tried to teach them to dance, they never quite got it!!

They fell in love with the pastors, who welcomed them there, and learned things that were very different from what they were used to in other regions. The ministry organization with which they traveled to the Congo took books to give to the pastors who had arrived for the conference, but there were not enough. They never imagined that the pastors would react as they did upon learning that they had run out of the books. They thought that maybe those who did not receive a book would gracefully say, "What a disappointment, but thank you anyway. We understand." But it didn't turn out that way! Those who did not receive a book before they ran out, began to shout at Ralph as he stood in the pulpit. They were so angry that it forced him to get down behind the pulpit to protect himself from them as they all ran towards him complaining about not receiving the promised copy of the book. But one has to understand the desperation in which they live and their reaction to a lost opportunity.

This was a unique learning experience that Ralph will never forget. His heart is full of compassion for them in their extreme poverty and desire to learn all they can to better their situation. The lesson was so well learned and came into play on another occasion when he took a minister with him to teach at a conference with the same group of pastors.

At one point in the event, Ralph had to leave to do an errand elsewhere in the city. While driving Ralph to his appointment, his chauffeur told him that the pastor whom Ralph had left behind to teach in the conference planned to give away twenty dollars to anyone who dared to come forward to help him make an illustration in his message. "Are you sure he plans to do that?" Ralph asked with concern. As soon as he confirmed that the guest teacher was indeed going to do that, he told the driver to quickly take him back to the conference. It's that Ralph remembered the books!

When he arrived, the pastor was in the pulpit teaching and had not yet offered the twenty dollars. Ralph ran to the pulpit and said in his ear, "Don't do the twenty-dollar thing." The pastor looked at him strangely but accepted the advice. Knowing the reaction to the shortage of books, Ralph did not even want to think about how seven thousand pastors would run to the front to claim their twenty dollars.

God gave them, even in other cultures, experiences that have served to guide, protect, and help others avoid problems, while at the same time, and with great compassion, understanding the challenges and needs of each country.

Riots in Kinshasa

Donna was very frightened that day. The men had gone out to do another activity, and she had said, "I'd rather stay here at the hotel; I need to go to the business center and check emails." This was before the time that they traveled with laptops and cell phones. For that reason, she had to go to the business center of the hotel where they were staying in Kinshasa, Democratic Republic of the Congo. Suddenly, as she at a computer with a window view to the street, she saw a scene totally frightening and dangerous. A large crowd of people was running in a noisy demonstration in the street. Their fists were in the air, and they were screaming. She had no idea what it was about, but the street was full of people running, yelling, and threatening over some issue. The danger was made real to her when she realized that she was in full view of all of them because she was seated in the window of the business center and facing the street.

She got up from the computer and did not take time to pay the bill or close her email. She realized that she had to run! And, run she did! She went up the elevator, got to her room and locked herself in the room, scared and waiting for Ralph's return. What a moment! She thought, "If those protesters see an unaccompanied and helpless American woman, who knows what they could have done in such fury?" Ralph returned with the rest of the men on the team and Donna told him what had happened. They confirmed that there had been unrest in the city. It was a real danger, one more of the many experienced while on mission.

Resisting

At a ladies' conference in the states, Donna was among the speakers for the event. She had not yet ever gone to Africa, and honestly, she didn't really want to. Her desire to go to Liberia, West Africa as a teenager had been redirected to other parts of the world.
At that event, another of the speakers called her out and began to speak prophetically to her saying: "Donna, I see

you ministering in Africa, I see many dark faces in a remote place, with thatch huts like those common to Africa." To that Donna replied: "We have ministered in Haiti, and it looks like an African country. Could that be what you are seeing?" "No," she said, "I see you in Africa."

After a few months, Donna received an invitation to accompany Ralph to the Congo to participate in the previously mentioned conference. It was amazing. Thousands of pastors had gathered for the event. At the close of the conference, the director of the event told Donna: "Pastor, the women are asking for a day for them; would you be able to minister to them tomorrow?" Of course, Donna answered in the affirmative. That day, seven hundred women gathered in an incredibly small room. They were literally shoulder to shoulder. The challenging detail was that it wasn't just to speak to them. The director told her, "They will all want you to lay hands on them and pray for them individually." When she saw so many women coming in the venue, she wondered how she could possibly pray for all of them.

The women didn't speak English, but with a translator at her side, she organized them in a line to at least release a blessing over them. She began to bless them one at a time, although she later organized them into small groups of three at a time. She spent the whole day ministering to those seven hundred women.

That was her first experience in Africa, after having resisted a bit at the possibility. She later returned to Nigeria, Kenya, Uganda, and Zimbabwe. When God calls, His call cannot be resisted. When we walk in obedience, He gives us the will to obey Him and all that is required to serve in those difficult places. He calls you, prepares you, sends you and takes care of you!

There are many memories of the experiences in Nigeria, a country with a large population. There are more people in the nation of Nigeria alone than in the rest of the African continent. There are masses of people everywhere. It is chaotic. There are areas that are wonderful; there are areas that are dangerous and sometimes even ominous. But there, too, God has given them the grace to serve on a regular basis.

PAKISTAN

An armed guard

Often the call of God has taken Ralph and Donna into dangerous areas, but He always covered them with His protection in these ministry adventures. Ralph was in Pakistan. A Pakistani pastor invited him to speak into his ministry, which was very well established in that nation. On this trip, Ralph had to travel alone, and the times in Pakistan were very volatile and dangerous. Mob demonstrations, bomb blasts, and a very turbulent political situation were all in the news.

In the middle of all that scenario, and once he arrived at the hotel room, Ralph called Donna and said: "I'm in my room, I have the door closed and I placed a piece of furniture in front of the door to block it. There is a lot of danger right now. The host pastor has recommended another hotel to me, but I will not be able to change hotels until tomorrow." Donna gave her children the news that their dad had called from Pakistan, and that he was in his hotel and didn't plan to leave because of the danger. Tim replied, "If my dad is closed up in a hotel, there really is danger." Ralph loves to walk the streets of cities, be among the people and get to know the culture. But this time it was very different.

The next day, he changed to a more secure hotel and was at peace. However, in Pakistan, he had to remain on permanent alert because of the dangers that were many and varied. He was taken to the meeting venue, where he was to preach, in a van with closed curtains because they had said that it was not safe for an American to be seen in the vehicle. He had to travel with an armed guard, who told him each time they stopped: "Wait here in the van." He would go in the facility with his gun in hand to check out the whole place to later return and say: "Everything is fine, there is no danger, you can go on in."

Pakistan is possibly the country where Ralph has most certainly perceived the danger of being attacked. However, the certain danger that existed there did not prevent him from ministering with passion, with love, and with the same commitment. His activities included visiting a Christian school and ministering to the believers. Certainly, Christians in Pakistan suffer much persecution. Once people realize that someone has become a Christian, they are treated very differently by their society. They live a persecuted lifestyle, and Ralph saw that firsthand. His ministering and concern for them reflects a genuine love, a burden, and an immense pain to see them suffer as they do on a regular basis. Once again, whatever God calls you to do, and wherever He sends you, He will always equip you with the love that is needed for that country and people group. The Will of God will not take you where the grace of God cannot sustain you!

EGYPT

To the car, fast!

While in the city of Cairo, Egypt, Ralph and Donna had a once in a lifetime ride through the city! They had ministered in a very large church. The auditorium was so full that the people, for the most part, were standing and very attentive to the Word. The place was packed. No room for even one more person. Seeing them all shoulder to shoulder was exciting.

At the end of the service, the host pastor hurriedly told them: "We have to leave, we have to leave now!" They ran out of there like lightning to the car as the pastor yelled at them, "To the car, fast!" Once in the car, and at high speed, they crossed the entire city of Cairo with policemen escort in front of them clearing the way with their lights and sirens as if it were a president of a country or some important dignitary that they were escorting. A movie scene!

Cairo is a huge city, with a lot of traffic; however, they finally arrived safely at the hotel where they were staying. To this day, they do not know if the rumor that they were going to be attacked for being Americans and ministering in Cairo was real or not, but the truth is that the scare, for whatever reason, was real. They had never been traveling at high speed for forty minutes, escaping from an unknown danger, in any country in the world.

But on that same journey, the Lord used them to minister to many pastors at a retreat in the city of Alexandria, believed to be the city where Joseph and Mary took Jesus when the king's decree ordered that the babies be killed. In that historic city, they were able to minister to many Egyptian pastors, who pay a high price and live with persecution for being Christians. Nothing is easy for those beloved believers and friends. Thus, another chronicle from another land where Ralph and Donna were able to serve.

"Every day you can progress. Every step can be fruitful. However, a path will open before you that is constantly lengthening, ascending, and improving. You know you'll never make it to the end of the journey. But this, far from discouraging us, only increases the joy and glory of climbing."
- *Churchill*

RUSSIA

Beware of the mafia

The scares continued, and this time in Russia. Ralph and Donna traveled to participate in a leadership conference about four hours out of Moscow. The trip was made by car. When they finished the conference, they were able to share a good time with the other speakers from the event at the hotel where they were staying.

While they ate and enjoyed a chat, two mafia men approached their table and stood in front of them ready to attack. They took one of the speakers and pinned him against the wall while they continued to threaten him. Ralph's personality could not allow him to heed the recommendation not to intervene! Therefore, he confronted them face to face, as he had done on other occasions with others who were threatening or stealing from him. Ralph has his own way of resisting and confronting danger. He got up from his chair and went against the two mafia members to rescue his colleague, while another pastor shouted, "Careful, they have knives!" Thank God, at that crucial moment the security of the hotel made its appearance and rescued everyone from that danger.

That same night, and after that dinner at the hotel, they had to leave to take the train back from Yuroslav to Moscow.

They planned to travel during the night hours and arrive in Moscow at daybreak. They were accompanied by a missionary who lived in Moscow and spoke Russian. Because of her experience living in Russia, she readily realized that there were mafia members spread throughout different cars on the train. It is customary for them is to take advantage of the passengers while asleep, to threaten and to rob them. That is why the missionary, with great cunning, made the arrangements for all Americans to travel in the same car of the train where there were no mafia members to threaten them. She did have to be in another car, but knowing how they operated, she knew how to protect herself. She took the place of the foreigners and sent them to a safer car on the train. Ralph and Donna will be forever grateful for her life of service and experience.

Arriving in Moscow and having to travel by taxi from the station to the apartment, they realized that the driver was also part of the mafia! That's why the missionary, in a very low voice told them, "Don't talk." If they would have spoken English, the driver would have noted their origin as Americans. The missionary spoke to the driver in Russian. The tension level was high on that taxi ride.

But that wasn't all. Somehow, the mafia kept showing up the rest of the trip. When they were on the metro to go to the missionary's apartment, she motioned for them to get off at the next stop. As they stepped off, she explained, "This isn't really our stop, but I saw mafia on the train, and I didn't want to get off at my stop, because I don't want them to know where I live." Yes, they were everywhere!

Ralph and Donna's memories of Russia are not good. They felt a lot of sadness and danger while moving about in a country controlled by the mafia. While they were in the city where the conference was held, they were unexpected witnesses of a funeral. They observed a coffin being carried down the street in the procession by a mafia group while threatening their enemy, yet another mafia group. Suddenly a battle broke out, as some thought that the moment of the funeral was a good opportunity to take revenge for the death of one of their own at the hands of their enemy. Ralph and Donna could not help but notice the revenge in everyone's eyes. But they know that God's loving eyes and hands can change history. That's why they go!

ASIA

Another country that has impressed Ralph and Donna with its diversity and culture is India. It is the second most populous country in the world. It is divided into states or areas. For example, in South India where there is a large percentage of Christians, there is not as much persecution nor threat from the Hindu religion. But in other sectors, where the number of Christians is minimal, the danger is real, both for American citizens and also for Indian Christians. However, the Lord gave them grace to minister in that country and among that people group with so much diversity even among its own people. India is beautiful in many parts of the country, extravagance can be found, but the poverty is overwhelming. One cannot escape from an encounter with the reality of the extreme poverty in which millions of the people live.

Thailand, Cambodia, Indonesia

Being mission pastors in Dallas gave them the opportunity to send and help open areas of missionary service in Asia, including Thailand, Indonesia, and Cambodia. Those who were sent there opened training centers to which Ralph and Donna frequently traveled to teach.

In response to the need in these countries, they also opened rescue shelters and homes for children, many being children of mothers who worked as prostitutes. Rescuing children has its level of danger. It's another area of missions that remains challenging, as many still do not want to acknowledge that the need even exists. God has given to those with a call the opportunity to fulfill their passion to rescue many children from being sold, raped, and exploited.

Visits to these countries opened another gateway to understanding and working in yet another culture. In Vietnam, they experienced ministry in a communist country where Christians live persecuted and worship in secret. To teach a group of pastors in that country, they had to go to "a building" that was not identified as a church. They went up to the third floor. The believers met secretly, also checking for strangers to block them from access to where Ralph and Donna were teaching the Word. A lot of risk, but a lot of need!

Their hearts were touched and endeared to the people of Asia. Most believers are constantly challenged as they minister among Hindus, Buddhists, Islam, and atheism as is characteristic in Communist countries.

SRI LANKA

Trembling with fever

In Sri Lanka, foreigners and Christians are slightly more tolerated than in some other areas of Asia. It is a Buddhist country. There is less danger because they are a people more inclined to peaceful solutions, although the opposition can still be felt. This was also observed in Cambodia and Thailand.

On one of those trips to Sri Lanka, Ralph called Donna from the hotel where he was staying, trembling and very ill with a high fever. That was before cell phones. His condition did not even allow him to get out get of bed. He was able to reach the room phone, and through the hotel operator he connected with Donna who had remained in the United States. That was on a Sunday morning. They were in the church service and the call came into the church office. Thank God, someone was there to answer the call. They called Donna out of the service saying, "Your husband is on the phone and he's calling for you." Ralph explained: "Donna, I don't know what I'm going to do, I can't get out of this bed, I'm burning up with a fever, shaking and weak. I don't know what I'm going to do." Donna asked, "But what about the missionary who is with you?" "I haven't been able to call his room yet," Ralph explained.

But thank God, at that very moment the missionary arrived at his room and began to pray for him! Meanwhile in Dallas, Donna "interrupted" the Sunday morning service saying, "My husband is in Sri Lanka, he's sick, we have to pray for him now." The whole church began to pray! Strength came back into Ralph; he was able to get out of bed and prepare for the trip they were to make that day from Sri Lanka to India. A doctor who was there in the dining room of the hotel realized that he was very sick, so he helped him get some medication. A doctor?... for them it was an angel that the Lord had sent Ralph's way. "It's probably malaria," the doctor said. But thank God who healed him completely! Malaria is often a repetitive condition once contracted in the body, but he has never again suffered such a physical crisis.

ISRAEL, GOD'S COVENANT LAND

Another very important part of ministry the Hollands do with passion involves travel and visits to Israel. It was 1992 when Ralph and Donna were offered a free trip to Israel. Another pastor had decided not to go, which resulted in a vacancy and a need. The invitation included them serving in the group as *tour* pastors. Of course, there was a team already assembled, but there was a need to have a pastor present in the group. Donna, very honestly, said to Ralph: "I am not interested in going. I have taught throughout our ministry classes about the Old Testament and the Life of Christ. I don't have to see to believe, and I don't really care about seeing a bunch of stones, dry land and deserts." However, she knew that Ralph wanted to go. So, reluctantly and without much enthusiasm, she agreed to accompany him.

Donna had never crossed the Atlantic Ocean; they had not yet even traveled to Europe. This was their first transatlantic flight. At the time of that trip, Donna was still very fearful when flying. Usually, on her plane trips she did not sleep or eat because she was so nervous about the flight. On that flight to Israel, that exaggerated fear was taken away from her. She noticed that after that trip, there was a big change in her anxiety when having to fly.

Donna was going along to please her husband; he was excited about the experience they would get to live while in Israel. The truth is that from the very moment the plane touched down on the runway until the moment of their return, Donna was fascinated with the experience. Getting off the plane, they felt something they had never felt. Every night, when awake because of jetlag, she was studying her Bible and preparing for the next Biblical sites they would visit. When the time came, neither of them wanted to leave Israel.

It was an incredible, unique experience that marked their lives, not only for the many details of each historic site, but also for the possibility of "reading the Bible with even greater understanding." From then on, the Lord granted them the opportunity to take many other trips, which in Israel are referred to as "pilgrimages." One very enlightening trip was a diplomatic trip that allowed them to interact with the government of Israel, visit an army camp, get behind the stage at the commonly visited tourist sites, and thus get in touch with other realities of the country, in addition to everything biblical.

As time and opportunities to return to Israel became available, the desire to take others to that beautiful experience increased, which has now allowed them to visit Israel twelve times. When God gives an opportunity, their counsel is to never say, "No, I do not want to go." Take advantage of every opportunity to enrich your life.

Their lives have been greatly blessed with the God-given opportunities that they have lived. Ralph and Donna are somewhat different. She likes to know where she is going and all the details pertaining to that place. On the other hand, for him, it is enough that the opportunity is presented, even if not all the information is yet available. This fusion of styles has resulted in many journeys, including trips to Israel, that have become a significant part of the ministry the Lord has given them.

They have even been given the opportunity to provide apostolic covering for a Jewish Christian pastor residing in Jerusalem. That acquaintance was made in another opportunity when they were invited to participate in a conference for Christian believers in Beersheba, Israel. He was at that conference. Coincidentally, sometime after that event they encountered him at the airport in Veracruz, Mexico. There the pastor said to Ralph, "I was in the group in Beersheba, Israel, I appreciate your ministry." He then asked, "Can I meet you in your office in Dallas?" "Of course," Ralph replied. And from then on, a beautiful relationship began that has greatly enriched the lives of both. God's opportunities can lead to blessings that one cannot imagine. Do not hesitate, obey!

PART 6

PROCESSES

SACRIFICES

Serving the Lord and offering one's life involves renouncing many things. Although everyone knows that, not everyone dares to live it. Personal desires are left behind to embrace the things of God, His desires, His plans.

The only thing Donna would mention as something that she had to give up would have to do with a higher education and the opportunities that she did not accept to get a university degree. She graduated first in her high school class; she gave the valedictorian speech at her graduation. Her professors did not understand why she insisted on going to a Bible college, when she could have gone to any university with a full scholarship. She probably would have chosen the path to become a lawyer. That was her greatest interest as far as a career. Without a doubt, she would have been a great law student and would today be a lawyer. But she knew that the Lord had called her to ministry and that it was His will for her to go to Bible college. Although she did not pursue a university career, she feels abundantly blessed and fulfilled.

Romano 12:1
In almost every teaching she prepares, she cannot help but mention Romans 12:1; a text that has been the foundation on which she has based her life:
"I beseech] you therefore, … that you present your bodies a living sacrifice, holy, acceptable to God, which is your reasonable service." (NKJV)

Reasonable service means that's the least one can do. It's not something one can boast about, saying "look what I've done." It is what is expected of a disciple of Jesus. That is why she is troubled thinking that someone could boast about any accomplishments for the Lord for which they would claim personal credit. However, if the chronicles of her life, together with Ralph, can inspire others to make that decision, to leave everything on the altar and follow the Lord unconditionally, then sharing these life experiences in this book will have been worth it to her. Relentless!

Of course, they have lived moments "by faith alone"; moments of scarcity in which they had to pray to pay the bills and to have food on the table, but the Lord has been faithful. It would be very difficult for her to say that she has made sacrifices to serve the Lord for the simple reason that she cannot imagine doing anything else but serve the Lord.

When they were in a denomination, they knew they would have their salary covered. They would be assigned to go from church to church raising commitments, "Partners in Missions" as they were called, before they went out to the mission field. But they knew that the denomination was going to take care of them. However, after leaving a denominational structure, when they returned to missions in 1988 as non-denominational missionaries, they knew it was a larger step of faith. They would no longer have a headquarters that would supply whatever they lacked. And in that new venture, they learned a lot about living by faith.

Between being missionaries in Costa Rica and returning to the mission field in Guadalajara, Mexico, they pastored amost four years in California. There they had a good income, they lived very comfortably since they had a church that loved and cared for them. They received that church with twenty-three people, and when they left it, there were around one hundred and sixty people in attendance. But when entering back into missions, obeying God's will, moments of sacrifice became the norm. But still, looking back, it is always clear how God has always provided. This allowed for a special time, even for their children, to learn to live by faith and see God's provision.

"Take all you want but eat all you take." Lessons in living a frugal lifestyle as expressed by Donna's father...
Edwin Judd.

A perfect combination of generosity and stewardship.

CRITICAL MOMENTS

After the surgery performed on Stephen, who from birth had never eaten by mouth due to complications as explained earlier in this book, he did not know how to take a bottle. That greatly frustrated Donna, knowing that the surgery had now made eating possible for him. Stephen had become accustomed to his mother feeding him through a tube and "filling" up his tummy. He was happy with life with his stomach full. That meant he would have to learn how to drink from a bottle.

Three days went by, and though he had successfully come through the surgery, he would not drink the milk from the bottle. This was a problem. Finally, Donna prayed like this: "Lord, he has survived this very delicate surgery, everything is working fine, he has to learn to eat by mouth. I'm not going to eat until I see my son eat, I'm going to fast and pray until he eats!" The result was not long in coming. After fasting and praying only one meal, she offered him a bottle and Stephen began to drink milk like any normal baby! Thank God, that was test of faith with a quick answer!

When Stephen was 12 years old, and while in St. Louis, Missouri, Ralph took him to the doctor to do the usual exams reviewing the surgery he had in Puerto Rico at ten months of age. This was done regularly to assure that his esophagus was growing as he was. When the doctor saw the results of the test, he said surprised: "This is very well done, I expected to see an image of something like spaghetti where they transposed the colon to serve as an esophagus in your son's chest cavity, but this is an extraordinary result. Where did they do this surgery on him?" "In Puerto Rico!" Ralph replied. "Dr. Pablo Rodríguez Millán did it with his team." "No wonder. That's a very famous surgeon!" the doctor replied. He added: "Last week he was here teaching all of us. If your baby had been born in the United States, chances are he would not have survived." Again, there was yet further confirmation of how important it is to follow God's will in spite of what may seem like obvious reasons not to do so. This serves as a confirmation that it is best not to wait, but rather to act immediately when God speaks.

PARENTS & GRANDPARENTS

As part of being a missionary, there was the responsibility of going from church to church raising funds to complete the budget for the time anticipated on the field. The term on the field was usually for four years. Going on missions meant not returning to the United States during their term. Many special family times like weddings and holiday gatherings were missed. During their early life, there were minimal times for the children to be with their grandparents. Perhaps the lack of contact with grandparents could be considered an important and very significant sacrifice.

On the first fundraising tour, Donna was about seven months pregnant with Stephen. They raised their budget in record time. Perhaps this was because donors took pity on her seeing her traveling and pregnant!

The next time they traveled for the purpose of raising funds was four years later, between their time in Puerto Rico and Costa Rica. They traveled from one side of the United States to the other, visiting one hundred and eighty-six churches in ten months. On Sundays there were morning and evening meetings, and many weeks, Monday was the only day they rested. They were traveling with their two children: Stephen, was age four, and Kami had her second birthday during that tour. They haven't forgotten the times when they arrived in a new city and found the church location, Kami, looking out the window of the car, would say: "Another church?"

After four years in Costa Rica, they had to go on yet another fund-raising tour. This time Stephen and Kami stayed with their grandparents because they were already attending school, but Ralph and Donna took Timmy, who was two years old at the time, along with them. They spent two months traveling without seeing their other two children because they were on the western side of the USA visiting churches. Two months without seeing them! Another tour took Ralph and Donna up into Canada and clear out to Nova Scotia. There were times when the children didn't see their parents, and longer periods of time while on the field, when they didn't see their grandparents. Perhaps they would consider this part of the price and sacrifice that went along with being obedient to the Lord's call.

"Finish what you start." Simple, but very important counsel as expressed by .
- **Edwin Judd** (Donna's father)

THE TRAVEL TRAILER

The tours they did every four years were intense and exhausting. They did require a lot of sacrifice. Going from church to church every night, saying the same thing to raise funds, taking along the children, being in the homes of people they did not know, other times in hotels, and many times in a guest quarters in the church. These were difficult times.

However, when they did the ten-month tour with two-year-old Kami and four-year-old Stephen, they had a mobile home that they pulled behind the car they were driving. It was new, quite large, had a kitchen, bathroom and all the necessary equipment so that they could sleep well and in their own bed each night. Once they knew where they would park upon arrival, they already knew where they would sleep that night. Mobile homes, at that time, were very comfortable accommodations used for family vacations and for traveling ministries.

Even with this convenience, it was exhausting to spend every night in a church service and every day on the road. These meetings were scheduled in different cities that were a comfortable driving distance to allow a time to set up their trailer prior to the meeting. But there were occasions when they had to leave immediately after the meeting at night and drive two or three hours, so they would not have to drive so far the next day. At that time the churches announced a special meeting when the visit of a missionary was confirmed. Forty-five years ago, receiving a missionary in the church was a special and highly anticipated event on whatever night of the week.

The truth is that every night, in every church, the missionary was expected to arrive with enthusiasm, as if it were the first presentation of their vision, and convincingly explain the reasons they were on the field, and all the while present the need for funds to sustain what they were planning to do. Although at times stressful and difficult, including living in the mobile home with two small children and Kami's dog, it was an unforgettable experience.

In each city, each church was a new challenge that required different and innovative strategies. Those were not the days of edited videos with graphics and moving details, but rather of posters, slides, projectors, and screens. Creativity was always needed to improve the presentation, create a connection, and to challenge the congregation to commit to ongoing monthly support. The messages delivered in each place were crucial to their ongoing missions support.

GOD OF PROVISION

As already stated in this book, if these chronicles from Ralph and Donna's life can inspire others to make the decision to leave everything on the altar and follow the Lord unconditionally and without pretext, it is worth all the effort. God had been faithful hundreds of times … actually, all the time! When Ralph and Donna were asked to share sacrifices from along their journey with you, the reader, they did not feel that they had a lot of sacrifices to talk about. They cannot imagine doing anything other than serving God with all their heart and being!

Giving of what God gave us
Even before they got married, they were already giving to missions. When they understood that they needed to give more, they increased the amount they gave. They began by giving generously. Soon they realized that it was time to give their lives and leave the comforts of the USA for the mission field.

One day, a woman who had received a substantial inheritance shared her powerful testimony with Donna: "When I was poor, I said to the Lord, 'If one day you give me and entrust me with a lot of money, I promise to be faithful to you and to give with generosity.'"

Donna really liked what she had shared with her. She accepted the challenge and promised the Lord that she would do the same. When the Lord began to bless them in abundance, she remembered the vow that she had made to the Lord, and that is why to this day they continue to live that commitment: "Lord, if you give to us in abundance, we promise to be faithful to you and to be generous to help with the needs that arise in the ministry as we are made aware of them." In response, the Lord's faithfulness has been surprising and abundant. One cannot out-give God. It's His promise, and He rewards the cheerful giver.

PART 7

PASTORING

MENTORING

Identifying gifting and training others has been a major focus of Ralph and Donna's ministry. They have been given hundreds of opportunities to identify those who are gifted and called to ministry. Training them, walking alongside them, serving, encouraging them, counseling with them, and launching them into ministry is their calling. Perhaps that is why, and although they do not much like to use the title, they are seen and recognized as apostles. For them, if someone is an apostle, they must have started by planting churches and raising up an effective ministry. They dislike the concept that someone can be an apostle in title only.

Ralph and Donna consider that an apostle is not someone who flies high over others, criticizes them, and makes demands on them, but rather one who goes before others and says as the apostle Paul said: "Follow me, as I follow Christ." As Jesus called his disciples, "Follow me and I will make you fishers of men." That has been Ralph's style. That has been his calling. That's his strength. "Follow me, as I give my life to follow Jesus Christ." Ralph wants to guide, not command. Guide others with what he has learned, the good and the bad, the right decisions and mistakes, the successes and failures. His desire, his calling, is to serve as a mentor to others through his ministry. Perhaps that's why many seek him out for guidance in their ministries.

In their ministry they have raised up many churches and Bible schools. Converts have been schooled and trained and sent out to their ministries. For them the apostolic ministry is not carrying a higher calling than others, much less becoming a celebrity, but it implies being with others, walking with those who do ministry to encourage them, to instruct, train and sustain them.

CROSS - CULTURE

Together with the apostolic ministry, the Lord gave them a grace to connect with different cultures in different parts of the world. They have built relationships, not only in the international events they have organized, but also in their missionary journeys and the countless invitations received from other ministries in different countries. It has been significant how the Lord has helped them to relate to pastors and leaders in their own contexts of life, culture, environment, customs, and forms of communication. Such has been the case in communities as diverse as India, Russia, Africa, Cambodia, Vietnam, Spain and all the Americas.

Being very objective, it can be noted that the key to Ralph and Donna's relationships with such a diverse pastoral and leadership community is a result of how comfortable leaders feel when with them. Others realize that they are not only there on location with them – but very approachable, identifying with them in each of life's situations. Leaders in their network know that it is not about the Hollands sending them material blessings, but rather about serving them in everything; not to condemn their style of leadership or lifestyle, but to identify with them, with their challenges, their problems, their need for answers, their cultural demands, and the circumstances of the pastoral task. They will never be able to respond to everything that is asked of them, but they will always give everything they can to serve in each situation.

They went to the mission field when they were very young, which allowed them to identify early on their unique ministry style and goal. The premise was and is: to serve from their own realities. It is not a ministry that was formed in their home country, the United States, but began in foreign countries, some very distant, where the Lord sent them to be missionaries. For this, the ability to relate was a fundamental requirement.

Ralph has visited more than one hundred countries of the world: Donna, perhaps, about eighty countries. And in each of them they strove to identify with the people, their leaders, their pastors, and thus try to serve them, help them, and encourage them in the Kingdom mandate to preach the gospel in all nations.

"The best time to plant a tree was twenty years ago.
The second-best time is now."
- *Chinese Proverb*

NEW CHALLENGES

No one will ever be able to prevent transitions from coming in their lives. Simply no one. An important mentor for Donna once said, "When challenges come, we have options. We have the choice to fight them and feel anxious or face them and wisely proceed with prayer, courage strategy and grace through them." Usually, people resist transitions, but that mentor was right. There are options available to carry us through the challenges. They are necessary and they are inevitable, so depending on how we decide to act in the transition times will determine the outcome: anxiety or peace.

Ralph and Donna learned that transitions should not be resisted, especially when they are part of God's plan and will. Transitions can be planned, or they can come unexpectedly. The truth is that when the time comes, prayer, courage, strategies, and God's grace will make it possible to enjoy the transition process with confidence that He is in control.

A special and decisive time came when Ralph and Donna decided to transition the pastorate of the mother church, the central church of Mundo de Fe, to Tim and Abigail, their youngest son and daughter-in-law. No one denies that transition is part of life's processes. Life consists of developmental stages like a child becoming a teenager, then a young person, then an adult. It involves leaving something to do something else. Leaving one place to live in another. Hand over the church they had founded, to found new ventures and ministries.

It is understandable that it happens, however the process is challenging. Donna had a little more apprehension and anxiety because of the insecurity she felt about her upcoming ministry involvements. But Ralph and Donna were both very confident in what they were doing and had complete trust in Tim and Abigail, in their calling, their dedication, their service, and their ability to lead the church to another level.

When they made the transition from being pastors of the central church to enter full time into apostolic ministry, for some time Donna did not perceive herself as an active part in the new arena. She considered herself a pastor and teacher. In those roles she found comfort, satisfaction, and fulfillment in ministry.

But as expected, the Lord worked with her and gradually proved to her that this was the new role He required of both of them. So much so that now, the difficult thing for them would be to return to being pastors of a local church. God had everything settled, everything in His time. Ralph and Donna found their new place in their new anointing, and that makes them highly effective and happy. As a couple working together in ministry, the challenge is to walk together helping each other to embrace the new opportunities that a transition presents.

"You have what it takes to finish what you started. Don't give up. The finish line is closer than you think."

ORGANIC NETWORKING
(As shared by the Hollands in Destiny Magazine)

Building an apostolic network should be organic, not manipulated.

Never would we have dreamed that close to 300 Pastors and ministries would look to us for leadership: a paternal leadership. We are honored to serve leaders with transparency and integrity.

Pastors and ministers are looking for someone that can connect them with a network family where they can identify and be encouraged. They are looking for fatherhood, mentoring, and encouragement from someone that has gone a little ahead of them and can coach them from the position of experience and from the Word of God. We strategically host pastors' conferences and training seminars in many countries as well as the USA. We always endeavor to be inclusive providing a safe environment for dialogue and that "pat on the back" so needed by so many. ***Organic!***

Over the past 50 plus years, God has ordered our steps, taking us to more than 100 nations through relationship building. Our networks, *INTERNATIONAL MISSIONS*

NETWORK, and MUNDO DE FE MINISTRIES embrace many language groups and cultures.

In the unique apostolic ministry that God has allowed us to serve, it has required understanding, embracing, and relating with different language groups and cultures all over the world. From country to country there are idiosyncrasies that require one to have the language, understand the history, work with government restrictions unique to each setting, and relate to the economic possibilities with the goal that every church eventually becomes autonomous while staying connected to colleagues in their region. God has given us an uncanny ability to do just that as we provide apostolic leadership. ***Organic!***

How did all of this come about? A little of our story goes like this. As a very young couple (23 and 21 years of age) we began our missions ministry in 1971 in the Caribbean. Ministry took us to Haiti (with its unique French/African culture and extreme poverty), the Dominican Republic (a Spanish-speaking country), St Marteen (a French and Dutch island), St Croix and other islands of the Caribbean. This region was the beginning of our training to jump from one culture and language group to another without pause and immediately identify with each upon landing in their country.

Later, during our 8 years in Costa Rica, we established a strong central church, a Bible training center and effectively placed national leaders in strategic locations to plant 17 churches.

Our next foreign residence was in Guadalajara, Mexico. This time in Mexico marked a dramatic change in our ministry role from traditional missionaries to an international ministry of networking as had been declared over us in prophetic and wise counsel. The word over us was that we would come and go from nations all over the world. At the time, it seemed impossible, but God had it all in His plan. ***Organic!***

It was in the next transition that we saw the plan of God begin to be fulfilled. The seeds sown in our years of foreign involvement all contributed to our new role upon setting up our ministry base in Dallas. *Organic!* We began to serve in a ministry capacity that would give us the opportunity to empower, send and coach persons and ministries that would go to many nations of the world. Through our International Missions Network, we continue to be a sending agency and provide oversight to national leaders and missionaries in Spain, Turkey, China, Russia, Czech Republic, Thailand, Turkey, India, Nigeria, Kenya, Israel, Honduras and Brazil.

Our time in Dallas also resulted in the founding of a large Spanish-speaking congregation based in the Dallas area. This church dove-tailed with our international calling to become the central church that would initiate and cover churches in many nations of Latin America. *Organic!*

A large ministry was founded in Nicaragua that has literally impacted and connected hundreds of pastors cross-denominationally and resulted in an example church being established.

In Mexico, the network of Mundo de Fe pastors crisscrosses the nation with the central church in Mexico City and many other churches that have started from that one central church. Some of our network pastors have been born out of our churches, others have asked to become a part, others head their own networks but feel the need to connect their smaller networks to our covering. Organic!

The Mundo de Fe Ministries network covers pastors in Mexico, Nicaragua, Costa Rica, El Salvador, Colombia, Venezuela, Peru, Argentina, Chile, the Dominican Republic, Cuba, Spain, and in many states here in the USA. One of the ministries that we cover in Spain also has churches in Portugal, Germany and England. The network also includes a pastor in Jerusalem who is a Peruvian Jew.

Our current role as apostolic covering and networking

allows us to freely "come and go" to encourage and coach awesome ministries in Latin America, Europe, Africa and Asia. Organic!

"Old age is like everything else. To be a success,
you must start young."
- *Theodore Roosevelt*

PART 8

IN CONCLUSION

JUST DO IT!

The Nike logo is challenging: "Just do it." That has been a trademark of Ralph and Donna's ministry. In many moments it all came down to doing or not doing what the Lord asked of them. No detours, no excuses, no pretexts, no conditions, no complaints, no whims. They just had to do it!

Waiting for the ideal time, and for so many things to come into place, often serves as a pretext and many times only delays what should be done immediately. Yes, just do it! The moment the Lord puts it in your heart and opens the doors, you should act. Do you have a call from God? Act now, obey now and don't wait any longer.

There is a cost, but the Lord gives more than we give. He is not indebted to anyone; whatever sacrifice you make, the Lord covers with His blessing. Always try to see God's blessing in everything. Don't count the sacrifice or what may cause momentary discomfort, but rather what you receive in return. Just do it. Simply and without delay!

"You talk a lot, you complain too much, you complicate everything.
Be silent and do what you have to do."

LIVE IN OBEDIENCE

Ralph's more active and adventurous personality made it faster and easier for him to obey and leave "for the unknown" than it was for Donna. She likes to think, plan things well, know where she is going, and when and with what means. But thank God that "the lady with a plan" walked alongside the "adventurous man," because the result is a ministry that has managed to plan its adventures in an inspiring way. Their lives are exciting! They have supported each other and that always encouraged them to take new leaps of faith. Everything has been a learning process. The need to have a fixed income bowed to a life of walking by faith and the result is amazing. It would have been in vain to put prerequisites and requirements on the Lord. Everywhere they have served, their requirements have never been extravagant, their requirements are always minimal, and sometimes they just do without.

When the decision was made to send them from Puerto Rico to Costa Rica, all they asked for was "to feel the peace of God in the decision to move to another country." That was the only requirement. The rest, God would provide . . . so they just went for it! Sometimes Donna's faith was not like Ralph's, "but I will go by your side, the faith is yours, but I will cooperate; and if I don't understand something now, I will understand it later. I will accompany you, let's go together," she told him. The Lord honored this attitude and will continue to do so with all those who, having faith, demonstrate it in only one way: by obeying. Uniquely in her wedding vows, Donna repeated the words of Ruth, "Wherever you go, I will go. Wherever you lodge, I will lodge . . ." Little did she know what that would entail, but she has never regretted that vow.

"Faith does not complicate life, it always facilitates it.
Obedience is the first step that faith demands. "

LIVE IN HOLINESS

There was a song that became part of Ralph and Donna's life, which said:

> If I live a holy life, shun the wrong and do the right,
> I know the Lord will make a way for me."

And that is the high standard for their lives. Paying the price of living in holiness, of walking a life consecrated to him unconditionally, was not for them an option but rather a requirement.

There was an elderly counselor who impacted their lives when he said, "The secret of holy living is living holy in secret." Wow! They have tried to live transparently and consistently. Circumstances do not alter who they are. Example and accountability are important to them. Everywhere, they try to live a life that pleases the Lord. Not with religiosity but rather with an understanding of God's grace and mercy. They are the first to admit that they have made mistakes. But God's grace gives us what we don't deserve, and His mercy detains what we do deserve.

Their great desire is to guide all those with whom they share their life to also live with commitment. It is possible to live a life completely consecrated to the Lord without the bondage of legalism and yet with deep commitment. The greatest authority of life rests in being genuine, in renouncing a double standard, being the same everywhere, being holy, being different in such a way that people can see in one the life of Christ and follow it.

"To be holy is to be different, to live with authority."

LIVE BY PRINCIPLES

A principle of enormous importance while raising their children, was to prepare them to make their own decisions based on principles. Decisions should be based on principles that one has learned and not on a list of regulations. The dictionary defines a principle as "a set of values, beliefs, norms, which guide and regulate a person's life"; on the other hand, a regulation is a "set of rules that regulate an activity." The principles are practiced by the person by his own convictions, while a regulation is a rule that is imposed on someone by another.

For example, in Donna's experience as a child, if she asked her parents permission to participate in an activity that she wanted to do, instead of saying "yes" or "no," they would start by dialoging with her. Before the conversation ended, Donna had already made the right decision. Why? Because they based those conversations on principles, rather than regulations. That prepared her to enter adult life when she was very young. She got married as a young woman because she was ready, that is, she had already learned a lot about how to make correct decisions and live with principles useful for all circumstances in life. Ralph and Donna applied these same principles with their children, and it has served them in their lives. There was little need for strong corrective discipline in their home because they determined to train their children imparting to them basic and Godly principles.

> "Don't be the slave to your own rules. Do not be the oppressor of those who cry out to be free."

PARENTAL INFLUENCE

A release to do the will of God was well imparted in Donna's life from a young age in times at the altar and times of consecration. Her father laid out many challenges, especially to young people to devote their lives to missions. When he saw his own daughter at the altar along with other young people, he would speak to their parents saying, "You may be concerned to see your teenager here at the altar offer their life to the Lord to serve in missions on the other side of the world, but I prefer that my daughter be on the other side of the world in God's will rather than living next door to me outside of God's will." Incredible! Wonderful! So, from a very young age she knew that her parents were not going to oppose her call to missions, in fact, they encouraged her, because they saw the importance of each one fulfilling God's purpose. Parents can have a lot to do with these decisions in the lives of their children.

The most important thing in your child's life is that they fulfill their personal calling to serve according to their gifts and callings. Parents should not impose a calling, any more than they should oppose God's call in the lives of their children. That's what Ralph and Donna have always practiced with their children. It was not assumed that God would call them to mission ministry or a pastoral role.

For example, their daughter, Kami, was not opposed to ministry or missions; she always went and was supportive and an active part with a very good attitude, seeing each change as an adventure. She was perhaps even more adventurous than her brothers; she and her dad often made quite a team. But she told her parents when she was very young that her longing was not to marry a pastor. She wanted to serve in a church as a member, but she dreamed of marrying a professional man and living "a little more normal life" than she had lived in ministry and missions. It is important to support the gifts, ambitions, desires, calling, and purpose a child feels for their life and not have some predetermined plan for them.

"If I am a father or mother, it means that I am the greatest model of life that my children have."

ONE + ONE = ONE

Donna left her neighborhood and, as she pulled out onto the highway, did not see that a car was coming at about sixty miles an hour and in a position to hit her broadside. By a split second, she avoided a real tragedy. Miracle! After she pulled over and regained her composure, she continued on her way. Donna had only casually mentioned this incident to Ralph.

Interestingly, a week later, they were at a meeting where the prophetic word was flowing. Suddenly the prophet began to give the following word: "Pastors Ralph and Donna, the Lord saved Donna's life because He knows that what Pastor Ralph does, he could not do without her help and support by his side." Of course, it was very significant that he mentioned that. But the prophet went on to say, "When we see one, we see the other. They, Ralph and Donna, are one." Yes, they are a team, they have always worked as a team and that is partly what has allowed them to accomplish what they have. But what was striking about that word was that description: "When we see one, we see the other." Perhaps this description defines true teamwork.

"Beware, lest you shine so much with who you are and what you do, that you leave in the shadows those who live and serve with you."

JUST PILGRIMS

At the time of this book's release, Ralph and Donna have been married for fifty-three years, have lived in twenty different houses, including a travel trailer for a year, and hundreds of other places they have stayed while traveling to raise funds. For many years the Lord did not allow them to settle in a permanent place. They have always seen themselves as pilgrims who are only in the world fulfilling one mission: to serve the Lord wherever He calls.

It seems that the Lord kept them in "restless mode." They moved from one house to another, in part, because He didn't want them to find comfort that would tempt them to back away from their calling. On one occasion, Donna complimented a missionary, who served in India, on the beautiful blouse she was wearing. To this compliment she responded by saying: "I think I better give this blouse away because I don't want to have something that I like so much that it could distract me from the most important things."

Donna is not suggesting that one should take a vow of poverty. The lesson learned is to not put too much importance on material things thinking they will bring us joy when real joy comes from living our purpose, without distraction or being side-tracked by materialism. Our joy must come from serving the Lord. Ralph and Donna do not reject blessings; in fact, they embrace them, but never at the cost of not continuing in God's perfect will."

MUCH TO SAY

Donna began ministry fifty-two years ago, when the role and prominence of women was not so accepted. In fact, at one point the supervisor told Ralph, "I know Donna is very capable, but it would be better not to use her because she is a woman, and she should not be in a position to intimidate men in ministry. You are being criticized for allowing so much involvement on her part." Ralph and Donna were always "one" serving God. How do you separate what is one? Impossible! Surprisingly, at this time, the common thought was that the woman had little or nothing to say.

There was a time when the advice of a mentor answered a great concern for Donna who, at the time, was wondering how to respond to some challenges. There were some conflicts and issues about which she felt that she had some understanding. The mentor replied, "Donna, the problem is that you have your dad's mind; but what a pity, you were born a woman! Your mentality and understanding would be more accepted if only you were a man!" It was a way of telling her that she had a lot to give and to say, but there were limitations on the opportunity to share them.

The oppression of legalism has always been significant in terms of so-called holiness and control of women. This is exemplified in having the men well dressed and looking nice, but the women without makeup, without jewelry and living under other regulations to "maintain" a standard of holiness according to their definition. But thank God, He freed Donna from this many years ago. Along with this freedom came the freedom to minister and effectively use the talents that God has given her. Her desire now is to break that bondage of legalism off women and see them develop their giftings and callings to the glory of God.

Thank God, times have changed. Ralph and Donna have worked with hundreds of ministries that respect women and their service to the Lord. The Lord has given them a Word to encourage and help many pastors to come out of their limitations. If God is in the matter, one has something to say, and Donna says it!

"You have much from God to say; say it, don't be silent."

IT IS NOT ABOUT SUCCESS

I Peter 5:9 ... standing firm in the faith, because you know that the family of believers throughout the world is undergoing the same kind of sufferings. (NIV)

We are called to be strong, to be faithful in the midst of what may be suffered when obeying the Lord in ministry. All over the world, believers, pastors, and leaders go through situations of trial, pain, and suffering. Traveling so much has given Ralph and Donna an authority that comes from actually having been on location with hundreds of pastors and leaders who have gone through all kinds of hard places. They have encouraged with love, tenderness, understanding and empathy. They can say that they are part of that immense cloud of witnesses full of experiences and covered with marks, with scars, that in fifty years of ministry were left as evidence and testimony, not only for them to stay strong, but to give strength to others. Nothing like experience and what one has seen and lived.

In times where motivations have changed so much, in days where being successful is the dominant motivation even when it comes to ministry, to encourage someone who wants to simply be faithful to their calling, is a fresh wind that blesses the soul. It's not about anything else, it's about Him.

At the end of each day of service, when God's man and woman return home, their main concern should not be to count the new number of "likes" or "fans" they have added to their social networks. The objective must be to one day stand before Jesus Christ who will confront you with only one thing: whether or not you have been faithful to what He has called you to do.

Be faithful. Honor your calling by doing what the One who called you has asked of you. Be true to what is before you. Be faithful in all that you are supposed to be. Don't try to be more than what God has called you to be. Don't look for something different. If day after day you walk in God's will, day after day you will know what His will is in everything. That is why you will not need to go "seek" the will of God. You will know what it is. Do it with desire, with all your strength, and do not try to be more than what the Lord has called you to be.

Discover your gifts and understand them. Set your purposes. Know God's plan. Listen to the soft voice of the Holy Spirit and fulfill all that He says. Yes, be faithful in everything, even if it is little. The Lord will give you more responsibilities; but now do what is before you.

"Be faithful in everything, even in the little."

LOVE YOUR CALLING

Staying true to God's will has always been a vital decision for Ralph and Donna. That unconditional faithfulness is the result of the honor they feel being called by God to ministry. They deeply love what they do.

When one goes through seasons of tiredness and weakness, they can expect to be tempted to quit. What sustains those who continue is nothing magical, it is the promise of God in his Word. As it is well said in Isaiah 40:29:
"He gives power to the defenseless and strength to the weak."

When one feels weak and tired, God comes to give the necessary power to counteract "the force of weakness" that, among other things, tempts a person to abandon everything. Our weakness is the perfect environment for the manifestation of His strength, of His power. Not in vain does God's Word make it clear again and again, as in Isaiah 40:30-31:

> Even the youths shall faint and be weary,
> And the young men shall utterly fall,
> But those who wait on the LORD
> Shall renew their strength;

They shall mount up with wings like eagles,
They shall run and not be weary,
They shall walk and not faint. (NKJV)

This truth is perhaps the key that gives the title to this book: **Relentless!** Not by magic or self-effort. Relentless because strength always comes from the Lord. He is the giver of new strength. With it you can fly high again in life, run without getting tired, walk without fainting. These are all wonderful poetic ways to affirm that the best ally to not get tired and abandon everything is God who is attentive to give strength when fatigue tries to win the battle.

This is also referred to in Nehemiah 8:10 (NKJV):

"… Do not sorrow, for the joy of the LORD
is your strength."

What does this mean? That nothing is done out of obligation, with sadness or with a religious spirit, but with joy. Yes, with joy! So much so that in the presence of tiredness, sadness, or similar feelings, the Lord Himself says in Matthew 11:29-30:

"Take My yoke upon you and learn from Me,
for I am [a]gentle and lowly in heart,
and you will find rest for your souls. For My yoke
is easy and My burden is light."

Serving the Lord is a unique experience that, among other things, has a way to deactivate all those feelings that would discourage one from doing it. When He calls us, He prepares us. He never places upon us a responsibility for which He has not first equipped us. So do not be afraid to give your life to the Lord to serve Him with all love and commitment! He guarantees that, despite the sufferings connected to service, the tools created by Him for those occasions will fill our lives with satisfaction as we realize that we have achieved something for Him and fulfilled an awesome mission in our lives.

The key is that you remain committed to God of your own free will and not out of obligation. If it is out of obligation, it will resemble a kind of inconvenient "slavery" that says, "since I have no other option, I surrender." No. That is not the case. When someone wants to please you by choice, the result is voluntary surrender.

"If you love what you do, then you will always do better at what you love."

IF YOU ARE READY, GO FOR IT!

In John 21:7-8 (NKJV) a truly significant incident is recounted:

"... that disciple whom Jesus loved said to Peter, "It is the Lord!" Now when Simon Peter heard that it was the Lord, ...he plunged into the sea. "

Peter saw that it was the Lord and did not think twice, he threw himself into the water! Throughout so many years of service, countless were the moments when Ralph and Donna had to "jump." Usually, Ralph's adventurous spirit meant that as soon as he was sure that the Lord had spoken to him, it was reason enough to throw himself into the water, into the unknown, into the difficult, into what really requires faith and daring.

The rest of the disciples stayed in the boat while Peter jumped in. The fact that Christ was there was enough reason to throw himself into the risk and go to Him. If the Lord is there, Ralph and Donna jump and go after Jesus. Obeying the call has not always been easy, but neither has it always been difficult. Why? Those who are ready to jump when that is required usually enjoy more what they are doing than whatever suffering they may experience.

That was Peter, if Jesus appeared, he was ready to go to meet Him. Why didn't the others jump? Let's not waste time answering that question. They were all able to do so, but only one jumped. Will you wait to know and do what others know and do? Then you will stay a long time on top of the boat. A ready person doesn't have to enlist! Why? Because he is already enlisted! If you are ready, then you are ready. Although it seems like a meaningless reiteration, it is not. Whoever is ready, does not have to say to the Lord: "Lord, give me a moment. I am going to get ready to do your will and I'll be back!"

One must always be ready to do God's will quickly, responsibly. One can spend years enlisting and never jump into the water of service. If you are devoted to the Lord and to serve Him, then it will be easy for you to quickly obey whatever He asks of you. It is more about worshipping the Lord than what you are doing for Him. Many find serving God a burden because they are focused on what they do and not on Him. So, their works become just a job. Peter had devotion for Jesus, so he threw himself into the water. Dare to throw yourself into the water of obedience more often and more quickly.

It is not a question of being ready, but of instantly obeying even in that which involves taking serious risks, such as Peter's risk when he throws himself into the depth of that sea. If you are faithful to God, He will be faithful to you. Your spiritual growth does not come from the things you do occasionally, but from what you do consistently with passion and purpose. Therefore, do not waste any more time in getting ready. If you're ready, then jump in!

"If only you knew what is missed by living in the security of the boat instead of jumping into the waters of faith and obedience!"

THE IMPORTANCE OF A VISION

Ralph was flying from the United States to Costa Rica on the Honduran airline, Sasha, from New Orleans to San José, Costa Rica, with a stop in Tegucigalpa. They were already flying over the Caribbean, when suddenly they found themselves in the middle of an incredible storm. Lightning had struck an engine of the plane. In that he was in the window seat, Ralph witnessed the incident first-hand. The situation could not be worse. Panic took hold of almost all the passengers. The plane was still flying, but with only one engine.

Soon the pilot said: "As you have probably realized, we are flying with only one engine, which we can do, but we will no longer be able to land in Tegucigalpa because the runway is very short and is in between two mountains. To stop the plane, we will now have to use the brakes of the plane instead of using the reverse thrust of the engines." And he went on to give his disturbing report: "We must head towards Nicaragua," which was in serious conflict with Honduras over a soccer game and inter turmoil in the country. When they could already see the lights of the city of Managua, the pilot said: "Well, as you can see, we are over Managua, but the government of Nicaragua does not give us permission to land here because we do not have an agreement with them, so we will have to continue to El Salvador."

In El Salvador, there was a new and long runway that would allow them to easily stop the plane with just one engine. The problem, the pilot explained, was that they didn't know if they could get there because they were running out of fuel. So, they prepared all the passengers for a possible crash landing: loosen their neck ties and belts, take off their shoes, and know how to bend down in their seat among other recommendations.

A woman who was next to Ralph began to cry and pray, clinging to her rosary. There was a state of panic. Everyone was terrified. But Ralph, instead of being part of all that reaction, remembered a vision the Lord had given him when he was ordained to the ministry in 1972. Yes, he remembered a vision at the moment that this plane could possibly crash! Ralph's vison from the Lord occurred at a missionary retreat in Quito, Ecuador. The vision showed four scenarios or moments of his life and of different phases of ministry that were going to happen over the years.

At that time Ralph had seen only one of the four events fulfilled. The other three remained, so he said to the lady next to him: "Calm down, we are going to land safely." She replied, "How do you know, how can you be so calm knowing that this can become a tragedy with fatalities?" "Believe me," Ralph told her, "I am sure we will all arrive safely." And then he took the opportunity to tell her about the Lord.

When they finally landed, ambulances and vehicles accompanied the plane until it stopped with a wheel over the end of the runway and the rest of the aircraft on the tarmac. Everyone was celebrating! Ralph, looking at the lady, said, "I told you so!" Ralph knew that the other three events from his vision had not yet been fulfilled, so he was sure that the plane would arrive safely at its destination.

The first event that was part of that vision was a moment while ministering in Haiti. The second occurred in Costa Rica, just before they left the country as missionaries and when they had a big crusade. The third was in a large open-air crusade held in El Salvador. And finally, the fourth scenario is the one he is currently living with the apostolic ministry that the Lord has given him. The plane did not crash, and the vision is being fulfilled.

"The security of your vision must equal the security with which you will travel through life fulfilling it."

RECOGNIZE AN OPEN DOOR

The Pastor they worked with in Dallas said, "It's impossible for a person to be in two places at the same time, but the Hollands can almost do it." Of course, he said it in jest, but talking about a very noticeable characteristic in them and their passionate desire to fulfill every opportunity that the Lord has put before them, even if they sometimes overlap. They learned this very effectively when they worked in the Caribbean with the supervisor who was, at times, too demanding. He taught them that they should never underestimate the importance of an open door, even if it seems insignificant. That is why they have always been willing to go through every door, to take advantage of every opportunity, even if sometimes it seems to be a small thing or something that in the eyes of many was not worth the effort.

What to some would seem insignificant, has often led them to scenarios and situations much more relevant or important. The opportunities that others despised or the doors that others did not even look through, Ralph and Donna considered them, stopped in front of them, and even passed through them to see what was inside. What they discovered, many times, was not important to them personally, but it was important to the ministry, and that is what is most important. You don't value a door by its size, but for what may be hidden behind it.

They have long learned not to belittle simple encounters. Before moving to Mexico, they went to a conference where they thought they were going to contact important people and be in a large group of pastors. They came away disappointed because there were only around 30 people at that event. However, there they met some pastors from Mexico who became the contacts that opened Mexico City to them. And, because of those contacts today there are several Mundo de Fe churches in Mexico.

At the start of Mundo de Fe in Dallas, Ralph decided to invite Miguel Cassina to participate in what was only their second Sunday service. Donna worried about that invitation because she feared that a very small number of people would be there. And there were just a few. However, in that visit, Miguel gave a prophetic word that has been fulfilled and that visit opened the door to later support several ministries in Spain, a country very dear to Ralph and Donna.

Who would have believed that a small and humble beginning in Diriamba, would be the open door for the national ministry that exists today? That being Mundo de Fe Nicaragua under the leadership of pastors so capable and relevant in that nation!

Don't despise small beginnings!

"When you work hard and try your best, the doors will open."

DON'T THROW IN THE TOWEL

Part of the triumph of running this race of life and ministry without fainting, without throwing in the towel, without giving up, is putting aside the unpleasant things of the past. Ralph and Donna's lives have not been perfect. There are relationships that have disappointed them. Many times, they felt let down by people in whom they invested a lot of their life and in whom they had many expectations. They realize that at times, they have also disappointed those who were counting on them. To be honest, it is very sad to meet men and women who say, "No, no more. I tried and nothing went as I had thought," "I have been disappointed," "I do not have the strength to try again. I've already done my part, from now on I'm just going to live life, but I won't try again." It's sad, painful, but real.

One day Winston Churchill, the great Prime Minister of Britain, said: "If you allow your past to fight and argue with your present, you will seriously damage your future." And he was right! One must leave the past in the past. Yes, that immense number of things, of unpleasant events, even those things for which one could boast. One must not relive failure, nor successes, because both have already been, and are no longer there. Take new steps, forward and never backward. One must not regret the pain of the past nor rest on the achievements made. We have a future ahead of us. But if your past struggles argue with your present, there will be no progress, there will be no learning, there will also be no joy of having arrived, of having achieved. Did it work? Were you wrong? Did you fail? It is possible that all the answers are "yes," but do not allow yourself that quarrel between what has already happened and what must happen from now on in your life. *"The old things happened. Behold, they are all made new"* is not only a biblical text, but also a truth that will save your future.

COMMITTED TO THE CALL

Ralph and Donna's commitment and diligence in their calling has been shown throughout all these years. Fulfilling the demands of the call and doing the impossible to meet the needs of the people has guided them.

When they lived in Costa Rica, Ralph suffered a lot from strep throat. Sometimes when this ailment attacked him, he had to stay in bed for five or six days with high temperatures, tremors, unbearable sore throats, a process that often forced him to go to the doctor, be hospitalized and treated with antibiotics through an IV. These incidents were so common that on many occasions he could realize that he was going to get sick; his body "warned him." Still, he would tell Donna "I have to go see a certain pastor" or "I have to go baptize those people" or "I have to check on a construction project because I'm going to get sick again, and I want to do all that before I get sick." Many times, Donna would get a bit frustrated about it, but she could do nothing with a husband committed to his calling and the obligation to fulfill his commitments out of love.

This is not boasting, it is just describing the faith, love, and service of two missionaries who understood that if they said yes to God's call, it encompassed all their life and for all the years they live. A visiting missionary from another country said from the pulpit to the believers in Costa Rica: " I do not know if you understand the caliber of missionary you have." He added, "I have lived all my life in missions and have never seen missionaries with such genuine love for the people they serve as Pastors Ralph and Donna." That is very true and to recognize it is not vanity, it is only due honor. They served and still serve with an unfeigned love and that is easily noticed in their life.

> "We are not asked for anything unusual, only commitment to what we have embraced."

IT WILL ALL LOOK BETTER TOMORROW

1° Corinthians 13: 12 (NKJV) says: "For now we see in a mirror, dimly, but then face to face. Now I know in part, but then I shall know just as I also am known.

In these days of COVID-19, not everything looks clear. As Paul says to the Corinthians, Ralph and Donna also see in an imperfect way the days they are living today. They don't understand what the future holds for their travels and how they will function in the ministry God gave them. For many these are disconcerting days, but there is a powerful hope. Soon, "…everything will be seen with perfect clarity."

The years have taught them that this is not the first time they have not understood where they are, where they are going, and what God's plan is. No, it's not the first time. Just as yesterday, it will happen again today and even tomorrow. You will see everything with perfect clarity. Everything that is now known is partial and incomplete, but then it will be fully known. Ralph and Donna have lived long enough to be able to look back and now understand where they were and where they were going.

They can't forget that time when suffering a great crisis and thinking that everything was finished, an older woman, full of experience in the ministry told them: "Now it seems that everything is over, but one day you will look back and today's crisis will only have been a small detour, just a tiny moment in the immense trajectory of your life!" Although the reaction to this wisdom was to doubt, to question because they did not see a future, the older woman was right. That crisis is hardly remembered anymore. Why? Because it was just a moment.

Today you know something, tomorrow you will know it completely, just as God knows it and knows us. God can see the whole. That should encourage us. The challenge is to not ask God questions. The point is to trust Him, even if we don't have all the answers. Why? Because now we are seeing imperfectly, just some puzzling reflections, but by our faith we can hope and be sure that the day will come when the revelation will be complete. That is what Relentless faith will do. What little they see now is the fuel to expect to see greater miracles from the Lord tomorrow.

"If we cannot see everything, it is wise to trust in the One who sees everything."

"Soon this life will pass, only what is done for Christ will last."

RELENTLESS...

We have walked so many times
with only the power that faith gives.
We have walked for many days,
not knowing where we would go.
We have awakened in countries
of strange tongues and rare foods,
but with the same pains
and the same miseries
as the world in its entirety.
We did everything with simplicity,
everything had the mark of faith,
everything was impregnated with the aroma of
innocence,
and the power of obedience.
We did it all for a reason,
out of love for the will of the One who knew
us from the beginning.

The Lord watched us as we traveled,
when we were away
and even when a thousand times we returned home
believing, loving, and serving.
He was there when in our younger years
they said: Don't stop, you can go a mile further!
He is still there, now that the bones
are hurting, the steps are taking time
and the back is bending.

That has been our life,
one day flying, another day returning,
a few days resting,
hundreds of days serving,
and a lifetime just giving.

So, we were adding years and more years,
building stories, opening paths.
Knowing the bitter taste of failure
but also savoring the unique taste
of serving the Lord in remote and unthinkable places.
We are no longer young,
we now must walk slower,
but making a stop on our way,
the eyes are flooded, and the smiles are not hidden,
because of our gratitude
to the One who never tires of
loving, sustaining, and sending us,
that is why we are Relentless in our service.
It is the greatest honor we have ever lived.

Ralph & Donna Holland

Made in the USA
Columbia, SC
24 April 2022

59371122R00143